ORAL
COMMUNICATION
MESSAGE AND RESPONSE

Cover design by Robert Lee

ORAL
COMMUNICATION
MESSAGE AND RESPONSE

Larry A. Samovar
San Diego State College

Jack Mills
San Diego State College

WM. C. BROWN COMPANY PUBLISHERS
DUBUQUE, IOWA

Printed in U. S. A.

PREFACE

The traditional function of a preface seems to be twofold: to state the purpose of the book, and to describe the book in brief. *Our purpose*, stated optimistically, *is to help the reader become a more effective communicator*. In order to accomplish this purpose the authors have tried to cover those principles that apply to communication situations both on and off the public platform, while recognizing that the implementation of those principles in the speech classroom will probably have to be centered upon the public speech.

Underlying our philosophy of oral communication are three assumptions: (1) that ideas, language, voice, and action are all integral parts of the speaker's message; (2) that the effective message is listener-oriented; (3) that every communication situation is unique, thus precluding the formulation of universally-applicable "rules" of effectiveness.

We have endeavored to keep this volume brief for a reason that touches upon the basic philosophy of both authors. We believe that the student in an oral communication class can more profitably spend the greater share of his time in message-preparation than in lengthy reading of speech theory. We hope this book will be complete enough to provide the student with the essential theoretical principles while leaving him time to do the research and preparation necessary for effective communication. Furthermore, we hope that the brevity of our treatment will afford the classroom teacher greater latitude in his explanation and application of speech principles.

The arrangement and order of the chapters also manifest what we believe is the "student point of view." Materials needed for the earlier speeches are covered, at least in summary form, in the first half of the book. The more detailed analysis of materials needed for longer speeches is found in the second half of the book. Suggested speech evaluation forms, sample outlines, and audience analysis guides are included in the appendix.

We know that the reader will recognize that the study of oral communication is not commenced and concluded with a single course or with the reading of a single textbook. The study of oral communication is, indeed, a lifetime endeavor. Each time we wish to share an idea or a feeling with another person we face a new communication situation, the results of which should teach us something about the principles of social adaptation through speech.

We wish to express our indebtedness to the entire staff of the Speech Arts Department of San Diego State College for many valuable suggestions regarding basic principles to be included, chapter arrangement, and the philosophical viewpoint to be expressed. Much of our interest in the field of communication is traceable to the lengthy dialogues we have held with our students, colleagues, and teachers, in particular, Professors Alan H. Monroe, Karl Wallace, W. Charles Redding, H. P. Constans, Robert Cathcart, the late Dallas Dickey, and N. B. Beck, all of whom constantly stressed the need for all of us to understand and be understood.

The persons most indispensable to the completion of this text are our wives who found time to encourage us while restraining kids, dogs, and cats.

Contents

CHAPTER

I

COMMUNICATION

OUR VERBAL ENVIRONMENTS

The major question which logically confronts you at this point is, "Why should I take this course in speech?" As a history, chemistry, psychology or an art major you are justly concerned with the question of taking a college course "outside" your special area of interest. Most majors, in this age of complexity and specialization, need all the experience they can obtain in their selected field. So the query remains, "Why speech?" The answer, at least in its stating, is quite simple. WE LIVE AND FUNCTION IN A SOCIETY BASED ON COMMUNICATION. Through communication, of which speech is one form, we are able to "keep in touch" with one another. One is able to tell others, and be told, how one feels, what one knows, and what one thinks. Without the ability to communicate (speak, write, listen and read) each of us would live in isolation, set apart from our fellow man. The faculty of oral communication is virtually fundamental to our living process. Without speech we remain near seclusion, unable to communicate our thoughts, wishes, needs or feelings to family, friend or foe.

The ability to communicate through language symbols separates man from the other animals. Because of his ability to

1

use language man can draw from the past and talk about it. The other animals can not relate past experiences to one another, and hence can not make ready for the present or the future. This principle of TIME-BINDING enables man to pass on his culture to others, to know what has happened to earlier generations, and how to adjust his environment for future ages.

You need only take stock of your waking hours to see the amount of time you spend communicating with others. Various studies estimate that we spend an average of eighty percent of our waking hours engaging in some communication act.

Freedom of speech does not benefit us much unless we have the ability to speak with reasonable effectiveness. History has often been called the story of people and governments trying to resolve their problems. It appears that to date we have but two methods of resolving our conflicts: we can talk them out or we can fight them out. The method of bullets and bombs, although used many times in the recent history of mankind, seems far inferior to the method of words and reason. A democracy needs and utilizes the spoken word. We have, in short, answered the question of "Why speech?" Either on or off the public platform we use speech to function in our various environments.

Your Goals

The purpose of this book is to help you solve your communication problems more easily and effectively. You have been exchanging ideas, emotions, and experiences with others almost since birth; hence, you have been solving communication problems with at least some measure of success. No doubt you will continue to do so with or without the aid of additional formal training. But the chances are, if you are like most people, your communication activities have become matters of habit. It is only through conscious study and practice that you can improve your communication patterns, and it follows that you will improve from this study and practice only if you are motivated to improve. You must personally see a real need for communication if you are to gain and grow with this training experience. An attitude that reaffirms the axiom that SPEECH IS IMPORTANT

FOR OUR EVERYDAY EXISTENCE, will contribute greatly to what you take away from this training encounter.

THE COMMUNICATION PROCESS

To understand the nature and function of speech, we must examine the process of which speech is but one manifestation—the process of communication. We use the terms "oral communication" and "speech" synonymously in this text simply because a speaker is primarily engaged in communication—that is in affecting the behavior of others. We ask and answer questions, we take part in conversation, we exchange ideas in committees and we take part in class discussions; we participate in situations for which we are prepared and in some for which we are not prepared. In short, we use "oral communication" and "speech" interchangeably because THE SKILLS AND CONCEPTS OF SUCCESS-FUL COMMUNICATION ARE THE SAME PRINCIPLES THAT APPLY TO EFFECTIVE SPEECH MAKING.

What Is Communication?

In its broadest sense, the term COMMUNICATION includes all methods of conveying any kind of thought or feeling between persons. The telegraph operator is communicating when he taps out code meanings that are responded to by other individuals. Actors, artists, writers, and musicians communicate with their audiences by various methods including spoken and written words, actions, form and color; and audiences participate in the communication process by responding to the symbols sent by each communication source. The tired student who yawns in an early morning class communicates something to the professor and to those who sit around him. A smile is a communication act, and so is a frown.

Another definition that is closely related to the first suggests that communication is the process of sharing with another person, or persons, one's knowledge, interests, attitudes, opinions, feelings and ideas. Whatever definition is analyzed, two crucial and critical characteristics seem to emerge. First, communication, when defined as the process of sending and receiving messages, implies that there will be a response to the message. Thus, communication is a two-way process. Second, the successful transmission of ideas is dependent upon mutual understanding between the communicator and the communicatee.

The Ingredients of Communication

Although every communication situation differs in some ways from every other one, we can attempt to isolate certain elements that all communication situations have in common. Every time you talk to your neighbor, or every time you deliver a speech, these ingredients of communication are present. What are they?

The communication act has to originate from a SOURCE. This source wants to express himself—to pass on his feelings, to convey information, to give directions, to obtain agreement, to get something done, or to relate an idea. He has something *within him* that he wants to share with others.

The communicator's idea, which to this point has been privately held, is now ENCODED—that is to say, the feeling within him must be put into a code, a systematic set of symbols that can be transferred from person to person. The procedure of translating ideas, feelings, and information into a code, is called ENCODING.

The idea, now represented by a set of symbols, is the source's MESSAGE. The MESSAGE is the essential part of the communication process—the subject matter to be communicated. It is the MESSAGE, in written or spoken language, that is the symbolic representation for the SOURCE's idea.

The message must now be sent from the SOURCE. The carrier or medium of the message is called the CHANNEL. Channels can appear in such forms as graphic signs, light vibrations, and air vibrations.

Even though the message at this point has been "sent," communication has not yet taken place. For there must be another ingredient, someone to whom the message is directed, the RECEIVER.

For the receiver to understand the message, to react, he must *decode* or retranslate, the source's message, putting it into a code that he, the receiver, can use.

Let us construct a very transparent situation and observe all of the ingredients of communication in operation. Suppose you, as the SOURCE, are running for class president. You naturally want to secure all of the votes you can; hence, you have an idea to communicate. You are going to talk to a small group of students and try to gain support. So you want to produce a MESSAGE. Your nervous system orders your speech mechanism to construct a message to gain you the support you want. The speech mechanism, serving as part of the ENCODING process, produces the following message, "I will work hard to improve faculty-student relations on our campus." The message is transmitted via sound waves through the air, so the RECEIVERS can hear it. The sound waves constitute the CHANNEL. The members of the audience, or RECEIVERS, employing their nervous systems, find meaning in what you said (DECODING). They now *respond*.

We will return to these ingredients frequently as we weave our way through the principles and skills needed in successful communication. Human activity is, of course, far more complex than the procedures just described. Factors such as how well the communication participants adjust to the variables of communication skills, attitudes, knowledge level, social system, and past cultures of both parties will greatly influence the success of the communication act. The specific communication environment, as well as the occasion of the communication act, will also influence the entire communication situation.

The Nature of Communication

From this introductory view of the ingredients of communication we see emerging certain working principles which should be kept in mind.

1. *Communication is a two-way process.* More than one person must be involved in any act of communication. Speech writers, authors, and musicians may compose in solitude, but there is no actual communication until an audience has reacted to the composition.

2. *Communication seeks to elicit a response.* The speaker communicates to accomplish a purpose. He knows what reactions he wants from his listeners, and this awareness of his purpose helps him to determine what to say and how to say it.

3. *Ideas and feelings are the materials of communication.* They must be specifically designed to accomplish your purpose. They must be effective ideas, ideas that, in the judgment of those who receive them, are worthy of expression.

4. *Communication is a symbolic process.* All communication entails the use of symbols of some kind to express ideas and feelings. When you use language to communicate your ideas, you do not simply transfer them to the passively receptive mind of your listener. Rather, you cause him to develop ideas that are approximately, but never exactly, the same as yours. The degree of resemblance between the ideas you want to express and the ones your listener develops depends largely upon how effectively both of you, as partners in the communication act, have made use of language—symbols.

Words are the basic symbols in linguistic communication; however, nonverbal elements also play an important part. For example, the sound of the speaker's voice, his appearance and actions are often as important as his choice of words. Communication calls for the use of a highly complex set of symbols including both verbal and nonverbal elements. Improving communication entails striving for greater habitual skills in combining and using all of these elements.

5. *Communication is a "real-life" process.* The outcome of any attempt to communicate always depends upon how well you adapt to the environment which surrounds and involves that communication situation. Among the factors which you must try to keep in mind are the occasion which calls forth your attempt to communicate, your relationship with the person with whom you are communicating, your appearance, mood, character, and personality; the knowledge, skill and perception of the receivers of your communication; the most suitable style and form of speaking; the channeling system you use to bring that expression to your receivers' attention; and the response

from that receiver which will achieve your purpose as a communicator.

To communicate is to do more than just send words. To communicate is to adapt your whole personality to the effort of arousing certain thoughts and feelings in the mind of another.

6. *The receiver's response is the test of the effectiveness of the communication act.* If the receiver does not respond, there is no communication. If the receiver responds in an unexpected fashion, one can suspect a breakdown of communication. In speech, the sender of the message knows his desired response *before* he sends his selected symbols.

ETHICS—THE RESPONSIBILITY OF COMMUNICATION

The Sender

The act of communication carries with it serious responsibilities. Communication involves, in varying degrees, changes of behavior on the part of both the sender and the receiver. Ordway Tead, in his book, *Administration: Its Purpose and Performance,* observes:

> . . . the tampering with personal drives and desires is a moral act even if its upshot is not a far-reaching one, or is a beneficial result. To seek to persuade behavior into a new direction may be wholly justifiable and the result in terms of behavior consequences may be salutary. But the judgement of benefit or detriment is not for the communicator safely to reach by himself. He is assuming a moral responsibility. And he had better be aware of the area with which he concerns himself and the responsibility he assumes. He should be willing to assert as to any given new policy, 'I stand behind this as having good personal consequences for the individuals whom it will affect.' That judgement speaks a moral concern and desired moral outcome.

This responsibility is compounded as the group the speaker is addressing grows in size. In this day of the communication explosion one may well find himself speaking before groups ranging from a handful of friends to a large conference or convention. This social responsibility was never more important than in our own time, when television and radio facilities make it possible for a single speaker to influence the actions and the thinking of millions of people.

The power of speech to influence the minds of others has for centuries caused grave apprehensions about its use. The crux of the worry seems to be this: the means of changing behavior are so potent that, in the hands of evil or ignorant men, they may be used to induce an audience to act in ways that are unwise or unjust. Perhaps one of the most astute rebuttals to this position was written by Aristotle over two thousand years ago. In *The Rhetoric,* Aristotle asserted that the art of persuasion (changing behavior) was good in itself, but could be used either for good or bad ends:

> If it is urged that an abuse of the rhetorical faculty can work great mischief, the same charge can be brought against all good things (save virtue itself), and especially against the most useful things such as strength, health, wealth, and military skill. Rightly employed, they work the greatest blessings; and wrongly employed, they work the utmost harm.

In talking about the ethics of communication it is essential that we understand that the evils, if they occur, are brought forth by men, not by the processes of communication. The devices and means utilized by the speaker are indeed his responsibility. The issue becomes one of the speaker realizing that he has an obligation to his listeners as well as to himself.

There are a number of indispensable questions that should be considered each time you are the initiator of a communication act.

1. *Have you investigated the subject fully before expressing opinions about it?* In your speech class and in this textbook you will discover that serious research and analysis is an important part of successful, effective and ethical speaking. Because you should speak only from a sound background, you have an obligation to be silent if you do not understand what you are called upon to discuss. "I don't know" is a valuable and too rarely used phrase. When you do speak, you have a

duty to be morally thoughtful—to know what you are talking about before you try to influence the thinking of your associates.

2. *Do you respect the intelligence of the people with whom you are speaking?* The speaker should never distort or "re-adjust" the truth because he thinks the audience will not notice the distortion. Any misrepresentation can easily cause an audience to reject you and your cause. The audience's perception of you as a "good man" will greatly influence the success or failure of your communication act. There are volumes of experimental research indicating that what the audience thinks of you as a person can either hinder or aid your cause. Aristotle, Quintilian and Cicero, the great speech theorists of classical Greece and Rome, agree—the speaker whose prestige is high in the eyes of his audience has a better chance of gaining acceptance for his ideas than the speaker whose prestige is low.

3. *Have you been ethical in the treatment of content?* Half-truths, out-dated information, the lie, and un-supported assertions are all part of the "suitcase" carried and used by the unethical speaker. The unethical speaker seeks acceptance of his ideas but is unwilling to have them tested by the rules of solid logic.

4. *Are you aware that what you say will influence others?* As we observed earlier, you are altering and adjusting the attitudes and feelings of others. A constant awareness of this fact will allow you to re-evaluate your language and your goals.

The Receiver

As a responsible listener you must be alert to the ethical character of those who address you. It is useful to be aware of the propaganda devices that are daily employed. The Institute of Propaganda Analysis has defined the following forms.

1. *Name-calling.* This device, which is often employed by unethical speakers, attempts to give a person or an idea a bad label. It is used to make us reject and condemn the idea or person without examining the evidence. For example, you have heard people say, "This clearly shows that Mr. Smith, by his immoral actions, is un-American and disloyal to the principles of our great country." "The proposal recommended by

the school board is undemocratic, dishonest, and riddled with graft and corruption."

Name-calling has played an immense and powerful role in the history of our civilization. Bad names have ruined reputations, caused wars and sent men to prison cells. Be wary of the individual who uses name-calling instead of concrete evidence and logical reasoning.

2. *Glittering generality.* In this case a "virtue word" is used to make the hearer accept and approve the thing or idea without examining the evidence. We believe in, fight for, live by "virtue words" about which we have deep seated feelings. Such words are "Christianity," "freedom," "right," "democracy," "motherhood," and "liberty." If a proposition is "for the good of the people," or "will maintain the constitution," the speaker suggests it cannot be bad.

3. *Testimonial.* This technique consists of having some respected person say that a given idea, program, product or individual is good or bad without furnishing any basis for the value judgement. In many instances the "expert" is not even competent to evaluate the issue under discussion. Be on the watch for phrases such as, "My doctor said . . .," or "The President said . . .," for these, in many instances may be an indication that the speaker is appealing to you through testimonial. *Remember the issue, not just the man.*

4. *Plain Folks.* This method is used by the speaker who is attempting to convince his audience that he and his ideas are good and honest because they are "of the people," the "plain folks." This was the technique of the Red China News Agency when it described the United States action in North Vietnam as "attacks on the poor and simple peasants of Vietnam." Politicians, who must secure the "common man's vote" to win the election, depend on this device.

5. *Card Stacking.* This method involves the selection and use of facts or falsehoods, illustrations or distractions, and logical or illogical statements in order to give the best or the worst possible case for an idea, program, person, or product.

In short, the sender selects only those items that support his position, regardless of the distortion they may produce.

6. *Band Wagon.* This device implies that since everyone else has accepted a given proposal the listener should likewise do so. "Jump on the band wagon," "Be on the winning side," "Everyone is doing it," are all examples of the band wagon technique.

It would be foolish to say that these techniques cannot on occasion be used legitimately, but their unethical use should not be condoned.

A PREVIEW OF SPEECH PRINCIPLES

The Organization of Your Ideas

Effective speaking, whether to one person or to a large group, demands careful thought and preparation. In your speech class you may face the problem of having to give speeches in the first few days of the semester before you've had an opportunity to study and absorb all the principles which are treated in this book. For this reason, we shall briefly look at some steps you should take in preparing your first speeches. The steps of speech preparation to be examined at this point constitute the basic themes of entire chapters later in the text. The order of the steps is not nearly as rigid as our listing might suggest. You may, for example, discover situations where analysis of the audience is the first procedure you decide upon instead of an analysis of the purpose of the speech. But regardless of the order in which you consider the six items listed, a thorough preparation should include them all.

1. *Determine the purpose of your speech.* All communication is purposeful—it seeks to elicit a response from the person who receives the message. This reaction can range from enjoyment at one extreme to direct, specific action at the other. Do you want your listener to understand a concept, agree with a concept, or act upon a concept? Think of your speech as an instrument of utility—a means of getting a reaction. A considerable amount of valuable energy and time can be saved by

keeping your purpose clearly in mind. Knowing what you want your audience to do or feel will influence what you say and how you say it.

2. _Choose and limit the topic._ In speech class you may, on occasion, be assigned a subject area, but in most cases your instructor will let you make your own selections. In other speaking situations, outside the class, the same procedure is often found. You may be asked to speak on a specific subject or you may simply be asked to speak. In all of these situations the observance of a few basic principles will enable you to choose the proper subject and limit its scope to meet the demands of the audience, the occasion and your purpose.

a. Select a topic that is worthy of your time and the time of your audience. No listener enjoys hearing about a subject that he believes is insignificant and trivial. Talk about subjects, issues, and controversies that affect the lives of your listeners.

b. Select a topic that is interesting to you. Unless you are interested you will not be sufficiently motivated to accomplish your purpose. Preparation will be a tedious task and the delivery of your speech will mirror this apathetic attitude. But, pick a topic in which you're interested (or in which you can _become_ interested) and you'll find that the results are apt to be contagious!

c. Choose a subject your listeners will find interesting and/or one you can make interesting to them. Think about your listeners, what they like, how they feel, and what they know. The effective speaker can, by knowing his audience, select topics that will interest them and also adapt new information to their interests.

d. Select a subject that can be dealt with adequately in the time you have at your disposal. It is obvious that the subject area of "Peace in the World" can not be intelligently discussed in a five or six minute speech.

3. _Analyze your audience and the occasion of your speech._ We have seen that the listener is as much a part of the communication process as the speaker. A good speaker makes it a point to discover all he can about the people who make up his

audience and the occasion that has brought them together. He is then able to prepare, adapt, and adjust his speech to the specific communication situation he is to face.

The process of analyzing the audience and occasion is discussed more thoroughly in the next chapter. However, we may draw a few guidelines to assist you in your early speeches.

a. Learn all you can about the place where the communication will occur. The size of the room, its shape, and other physical conditions will affect the dynamics of the entire speech situation.

b. Learn the purpose of the gathering. Is it a regular weekly meeting of a civic club or is it a special meeting called to hear you discuss a particular subject?

c. Learn as much as you can about the people to whom you will speak. Knowing their age, sex, educational background, occupation, needs, and attitudes, will enable you to adapt your remarks to the demands of the specific listeners you are facing.

4. *Find the material for your speech.* There are basically two places to look for materials—within yourself for what you already know, and outside of yourself to discover what you don't know. You will soon realize that what you know, in many instances, may not be enough to accomplish your objective. In addition, we often are quite prejudiced in terms of the interpretations we give to our perceptions. Two individuals seeing the same situation may interpret what they see in different ways. It is therefore necessary to augment our observations with those from other sources. In Chapter V we will talk about finding materials in books, magazines, newspapers, and other storehouses of information. At this point it is important to remember that the successful speaker is seldom the one who "talks off the top of his head."

5. *Organize and arrange the speech.* Now that you have the ingredients of your message—the materials—you must arrange them so that they make sense to your listener. In most instances, if you are thorough in your search for materials you will find far more than you can possibly use in the time allot-

ted to you. You will therefore be faced with two problems. First, you will have to decide what material you want to use. Second, you will have to make a decision concerning the organization of that material.

The purpose of your speech is the determining factor in selecting and arranging the materials you choose to talk about. You will want to include the material that directly relates to and supports the main idea of your talk as well as materials that add interest to your ideas.

Arrangement of materials centers around the three parts of the speech—the introduction, body, and conclusion. The body of the speech should be planned first. This includes marshalling all of the supporting material designed to establish the central idea of the speech. The specific problems of selection and arrangement of the ideas which constitute the body of the speech will be discussed in some detail in Chapter VI.

The main assignment of the introduction is to gain the attention and interest of the listeners, to put them at ease, and to help them focus their attention upon your speech. The material you select should accomplish those objectives.

The conclusion serves to end the speech gracefully and in a compelling manner. It may take the form of a summary, an illustration, an appeal, a challenge or several other endings depending upon the purpose of your speech.

One of the chief organizational aids is the outline. It enables you to visualize your material in a clear and logical order. It lets you see what materials you have and aids you in sorting the relevant from the irrelevant. An outline helps you avoid the aimless, disorganized sort of thinking that is characteristic of many speeches.

6. *Practice your speech aloud.* If you desire to have your message understood and your purpose accomplished, you must practice aloud. You should deliver your speech three or four times before you present it to the audience. It is important that you avoid memorizing while you practice. *Learn* the main ideas of the speech, rather than trying to memorize, word for word, large sections of the body. Practice your speech aloud and allow time for changes if, after hearing it, you decide that you need to make alterations.

The Presentation of Your Ideas

In Chapter IV some very specific principles and skills will be suggested as a means of improving the delivery of your ideas. At this early point we shall simply suggest some general practices that will be useful as you begin your speech training.

1. *Have a good mental attitude.* A good mental attitude towards the presentation of your ideas will make the job of delivering your speech seem much simpler and much more pleasurable to you and your audience.

Don't be unduly alarmed about stage fright. Nervousness is a common trait among beginning speakers. But even the "expert" experiences shaking knees, wet palms, shortness of breath, throat tightness, or increase in the pulse rate. Perhaps the following suggestions may help to allay your apprehensions.

a. The realization that some nervousness is normal may, in itself, help to minimize nervousness.

b. The attitude that the "audience is your friend" will also prove comforting. In speech class you can be well assured that everyone is working for you.

c. Come before your audience fully prepared. If you have doubts about your speech and your preparation, it is likely to manifest itself in nervousness.

d. Try to "feel" confident. Don't rush through your speech; have the notion that you are "talking with your audience." Feel free to pause whenever you desire. Don't be too embarrassed if you find that some of your words are not coming out as you wish. In many instances you may be the only one to realize what is happening. Often times the acknowledgment of a "flub" will relax you and your audience.

e. Finally, nervous tension can be reduced by having some meaningful physical action in your speech. Try walking during your talk as a method of relaxing and releasing nervous strain.

2. *Be direct.* Looking directly at your audience serves two vital and necessary functions—both of which are briefly mentioned here but developed in detail in later chapters. First, directness adds to a lively sense of communication. It indirectly tells the listeners that you care about accomplishing your purpose and that you care about them. You know from personal experience that the speaker who gazes at the floor or out the

window reflects a lack of interest and a lack of concern for his audience and for the entire speech situation. Even in casual conservation it is helpful to look at the person with whom you are talking. Second, by looking directly at the audience you gain invaluable insight into how your message is being received. The successful communicator makes use of the information he receives by observing his audience and making adjustments based on their reactions. Whether you are talking to one person or a large group of people, your perception of their reaction and response to your original message (feedback) will play a significant role in selecting, arranging and sending future messages.

3. *Be physically animated.* Try to avoid stiffness and a rigid appearance. Your posture should be comfortable and natural. Many beginning speakers develop mannerisms such as shifting their weight from leg to leg and resting on the podium. These activities call attention to themselves and hence direct attention away from the speech.

Gestures are quite useful in conveying thought or emotion or in reinforcing oral expression. They increase the speaker's self-confidence, ease his nervousness, aid in the communication of ideas, and help to hold attention. Relax and be yourself and you will learn that gesturing comes naturally.

4. *Use vocal variety.* Just as movement and gestures help to reinforce ideas, so does the animated voice. If there is sameness of rate, pitch or key, loudness, and quality, we have full-fledged monotony. Vary as many of these variable elements of the voice as you can consonant with conveying the full meaning of your ideas and emotions.

Try to avoid unpleasant and distracting mannerisms such as "and-a," and "uh." These and other meaningless vocalizations call attention to themselves and detract from your message.

Good delivery is simply being direct, friendly, conversational, animated, and enthusiastic.

SUMMARY

In this chapter we have sought to introduce the fields of communication and speech and to present a few elementary principles as a means of providing you with the essential tools of effective speechmaking.

As a member of a society that utilizes speech as its major method of communication, you should be aware of its importance and its effect upon you personally. In personal and private life, and in the workings of our democracy, we use speech to carry on our business. Training in this vital area will enable you to live better in each of your environments.

Communication, in its broadest sense, is the process of sending and receiving messages. All communication involves the following ingredients: a source, encoding, a message, a channel, a receiver, and decoding. When these ingredients are combined in human communication certain working principles seem to emerge: (1) communication is a two-way process, (2) communication seeks to elicit a response, (3) communication involves ideas and feelings, (4) communication is a symbolic process, (5) communication is a "real-life" process, and (6) the receiver's response, or lack of response, is the best test of communication.

The responsibility and seriousness of communication is so great that the communicator must be of the highest ethical character. This means that he should know his subject, respect the intelligence of his listeners, treat his content in an honest manner, and realize that he is changing behavior—both his and the receiver's.

When receiving messages the alert communicator listens for various propaganda devices. Among the most common are name-calling, glittering generalities, testimonial, plain folks, card stacking, and band wagon.

In preparing his early speeches the student should remember to determine the purpose of his speech, choose and limit his topic, analyze his audience and the speaking occasion, gather material, organize and arrange his material, and practice aloud.

In delivering speeches it is essential that you have a good mental attitude, that you be direct, that you be physically animated, and that you use vocal variety.

SUGGESTED READINGS

A. CRAIG BAIRD, "Responsibilities of Free Communication," *Vital Speeches of the Day*, 18, (September 1, 1952), 699-701.

DAVID K. BERLO, *The Process of Communication*, (New York: Holt, Rinehart, and Winston, Inc., 1960). Chapters 1 and 2.

HUBER W. ELLINGSWORTH and THEODORE CLEVENGER, JR., *Speech and Social Action*, (Englewood Cliffs, N. J.: Prentice-Hall, 1967), Chapter 1.

HENRY L. EWBANK, et al., "What is Speech?—A Symposium," *Quarterly Journal of Speech*, Vol. 41, No. 2 (April, 1955), 145-153.

FRANKLYN S. HAIMAN, "Democratic Ethics and the Hidden Persuaders," *Quarterly Journal of Speech*, Vol. 44, No. 4, (December, 1958), 385-392.

KENNETH HANCE, DAVID RALPH, and MILTON WIKSELL, *Principles of Speaking*, (Englewood Cliffs, N. J.: Prentice-Hall, 1962). Chapter 1.

J. MATIN KLOTSCHE, "The Importance of Communication in Today's World," *Speech Teacher*, XI, (November, 1962), 322-326.

ALFRED MCCLUNG and ELIZABETH BRIANT LEE, *The Fine Art of Propaganda*, (New York: Harcourt, Brace and Company, 1939).

WAYNE C. MINNICK, *The Art of Persuasion*, (Boston: Houghton Mifflin Company, 1957). Chapter 12.

THOMAS R. NILSEN, *Ethics of Speech Communication* (Indianapolis: Bobbs-Merrill Company, Inc., 1966).

THOMAS R. NILSEN, "Free Speech, Persausion, and the Democratic Process," *Quarterly Journal of Speech*, XLIV (October, 1958) 235-243.

WILBUR SCHRAMM, *Responsibility In Mass Communication*, (New York: Harper and Brothers, 1957). Part III.

WILBUR SCHRAMM, ed., *The Process and Effects of Mass Communication*, (Urbana: University of Illinois Press, 1954). pp. 3-10.

ORDWAY TEAD, *Administration: Its Purpose and Performance*, (New York: Harper, 1959).

KARL R. WALLACE, "An Ethical Basis of Communication," *The Speech Teacher*, Vol. 4, No. 1 (January, 1955), pp. 1-9.

CARL H. WEAVER, and W. L. STRAUSBAUGH, *The Fundamentals of Speech Communication*, (New York: American Book, 1964).

II

PRELIMINARY CONSIDERATIONS

YOUR FIRST SPEECHES

In general, it may be stated that most speaking situations are initiated because the speaker wants to achieve some pre-conceived purpose. He wants something from the audience, and he communicates in order to get it. Unfortunately, there arc occasions when the speaker does not clearly formulate his purpose. Obviously, if he doesn't understand exactly what he wants from his audience, he will probably get what he deserves!

The successful speaker decides upon and clarifies his purpose before he sends his message. By deciding upon the response he wants from his audience he can better select the ideas, the organizational patterns, the language, and the delivery methods that will enable him to reach his goal. The salesman that comes to your door may present an interesting talk with countless pieces of practical information, but his ultimate purpose is to persuade. Unless the materials contained within his speech are aimed at securing his purpose, he will not make his sale.

FORMULATING A GENERAL PURPOSE

The classification of speech purposes has long been a subject of controversy among rhetoricians and teachers of communication. Since ancient times disagreements have arisen over the number and the nature of these purposes. However, critical study of the historical arguments leads us to conclude that there are three general speech purposes—TO INFORM, TO PERSUADE, and TO ENTERTAIN. These three purposes apply equally to public or private communication.

We should remember as we discuss these speech purposes that we are in reality talking about responses we desire from our audience. Any discourse concerning this topic must take into account the obvious fact that all individuals are different, and therefore what is intended by the speaker as a speech *to inform* may well *persuade* or *entertain* certain members of the audience.

Informative Speeches

The purpose of informative communication is to increase the receiver's knowledge and understanding of a subject. Informative speeches may also entertain or change beliefs. A speaker whose immediate purpose is to impart information often uses amusing or dramatic illustrations to entertain his audience, thus holding their attention. Moreover, information, even if it consists only of "facts," may lead to changes of belief and eventually to physical action, although such results may not be a part of the speaker's purpose.

In informative speaking, your main concern is having the audience learn and remember the information you present. The teacher talking to her class or the manager of a department store explaining the duties of a job to his staff, are both engaged in informative speaking. How much the listener knows at the conclusion of a talk is indeed the real test of the speech to inform.

Some examples of informative subjects would be:
1. How water is purified.
2. The organization of the United Nations.

3. The circulation of the blood.
4. How the initiative and referendum operates in our city.
5. A review of the life of John F. Kennedy.

Persuasive Speeches

The major function of the persuasive speech is to induce the audience to think, feel or act in a manner selected by the speaker. The speaker may want his listeners to discard old beliefs or form new ones, or he may want merely to strengthen opinions that they already hold. He may even want them to take some action. The saleslady uses the speech to persuade as a means of getting the customer to buy a coat. The man asking for a raise, the young college student asking for a date, the wife trying to get her husband to mow the lawn, the Red Cross volunteer pleading for funds, the teacher trying to get his class to study, are all trying to persuade someone to do something. An analysis of your own daily life will disclose the frequent need for effective persuasion.

The following are examples of persuasive subjects:
1. Final examinations should be abolished.
2. The use of seat belts can save lives.
3. The United States should recognize Red China.
4. Contribute to the Heart Fund.
5. Support your football team.

Entertaining Speeches

The third major type of speech has the purpose of entertaining the audience. We are using the word entertainment in its broadest sense to include anything that stimulates a pleasurable response, whether it be humorous or dramatic.

The speaker wants the people present to have an enjoyable time listening to the speech. He is not concerned that they learn a great deal or that they change their mind in one direction or another. Entertainment is the purpose of many after-dinner speeches and a favorite type of speech for the comedian.

Some subjects that lend themselves to humorous treatment are:

1. My first time at summer camp.
2. Eating habits of the American people.
3. The art of making television commercials.
4. Embarrassing moments while enrolling in college.
5. My favorite diet.

These then, are the three major speech purposes. If you know exactly what the purpose of your speech is, you will have a guide for your preparation—a reminder that each bit of material contained in your speech should contribute something to the accomplishment of your purpose. We shall examine each of these general purposes in greater detail later in the text.

FORMULATING THE SPECIFIC PURPOSE

We have already decided that the general reaction you want to get from your audience may be stated in terms of informing, persuading, or entertaining. But the particular and immediate reaction that you seek must be precisely formulated into a specific purpose. THE SPECIFIC PURPOSE DESCRIBES THE EXACT NATURE OF THE RESPONSE YOU WANT FROM YOUR AUDIENCE. It states specifically what you want your audience to know, feel, believe or do.

There are three requirements a good specific purpose should meet. It should contain but one central idea. It should be clear and concise. And most important, it should be worded in terms of the audience response desired.

When my general purpose is *to inform*, my specific purpose might be:

1. To have my audience understand the important aspects of San Diego City government.
2. To have my audience know how to apply a tourniquet.
3. To have my audience understand the fundamentals of water-skiing.

If my general purpose is *to persuade,* my specific purpose might be:

1. To get the audience to give to the Community Chest drive.

2. To get the audience to feel greater allegiance to our college.
3. To get the audience to agree that we should withdraw our troops from Southeast Asia.

If my general purpose is *to entertain,* my specific purpose might be:

1. To hear the audience laugh at the "clear" statements of some political leaders.
2. To have the audience enjoy hearing about the best ways to stay out of college.
3. To have the audience enjoy, vicariously, my trip to Aberdeen, Scotland.

CHOOSING THE TITLE OF THE SPEECH

You may face a few occasions when you are asked to furnish a title for your speech. For example, when you are to be introduced by a chairman it would be helpful to have a "handle" for your remarks. A good title should be brief, should suggest the nature of your purpose, should be appropriate to the occasion and the topic, and should be interesting.

Recently one of our students gave a speech entitled, "Credit Cards: Bankruptcy Made Easy," in which she reviewed the growth of credit-card buying and high interest rates in the United States. Her title stimulated interest in her talk prior to the actual presentation.

CHOOSING THE METHOD OF SPEAKING

Regardless of your background, knowledge, or skill, each time you speak it is a different and unique experience. An effective communicator will recognize these differences and prepare specifically for each particular occasion. Included in his thought and preparation will be an analysis of the type of delivery best suited for the subject, audience, and occasion.

There are four fundamental ways of presenting a speech: (1) by reading it from a manuscript, (2) by delivering it from memory, (3) by delivering it extemporaneously, and (4) by delivering it in an impromptu manner. It should be pointed out that there are many speaking situations that may call for a combination of two or three of these types.

Speaking from a Manuscript

In this form of delivery the speaker reads his speech directly from a manuscript. In some instances this type of delivery is essential and appropriate. For example, on radio and television many speakers have to be accountable for their remarks and must be extremely accurate in what they say and in the amount of time they take to say it. Indeed, all speakers should be accountable and accurate, but the mass-media speaker has to be able to make instant referrals to his sources and materials. At conventions and business meetings the manuscript is helpful for the speaker who would like his speech to be circulated.

There are certain advantages to manuscript speaking in addition to those cited above. The obvious advantage is that it puts no strain on the memory of the speaker. His speech is before him and he need only read it. A second advantage is that the manuscript, having been written well in advance of the speech situation, enables the speaker to be very selective and meticulous in his style and choice of materials. The manuscript speech should be free from vague phrases, rambling sentences, and inappropriate colloquialism.

There are also serious disadvantages to this type of delivery. One marked disadvantage is that the speaker often loses sight of the importance of communication. He reads his remarks and many time fails to establish rapport with his listeners. The manuscript becomes more significant than the audience. When this happens all eye contact and all sense of spontaneity are forgotten.

For the beginning speech student trying to acquire the ability of sharing his personal ideas and feelings, the manuscript type of delivery is not nearly as helpful—nor is it likely to be as effective—as the impromptu and extemporaneous methods. But if you find occasions for the manuscript remember to: (1) write your speech for listeners and not for readers, (2) practice reading aloud, (3) remember eye contact and other techniques of effective delivery, and (4) concentrate on getting your *ideas* across, not just the *words*.

Speaking from Memory

The memorized speech, much like the manuscript, allows you the advantage of a carefully worked out and worded speech. Every single word is committed to memory and this, of course, frees you from the manuscript. One problem of the memorized speech is that this "freedom" often leads to mechanical delivery and the presentation of what often appears as a "canned" speech.

The memorized speech is also dangerous because one is apt to forget the entire speech. It is often difficult to recall the exact wording, and if you forget one word, you may forget the entire speech.

Even though the memorized speech permits a careful ordering of your thoughts and materials it should nevertheless be avoided by the beginning speaker. Training in the other methods will offer the beginning student practice in speech situations that more closely resemble "real-life" occasions.

Extemporaneous Delivery

The extemporaneous delivery is often referred to as the "middle course." The speech is *carefully planned, outlined, and thoroughly practiced,* but is not memorized. The exact language for delivery is not rehearsed. At the moment of presentation the speaker should recall only his organizational pattern, his main points, and his supporting material—in short, his focus should be upon ideas, not words. The speech itself should appear spontaneous and natural. In addition to a lively sense of communication, a major advantage of the extemporaneous speech is that it is well-prepared and carefully organized. This method is helpful to the beginning speaker in that it demands that he organize his ideas, that he think on his feet, that he speak conversationally, and that he adapt his speech to his audience. The shortcomings of the extemporaneous method are probably obvious to you now that we have discussed two other methods. First, the extemporaneous method takes time, and second, this method often encourages the beginning speaker to be lax in his language and rely completely on inspiration for his word choice.

A few suggestions might be helpful in trying to put the extemporaneous method to practical use.

1. Fix the speech in your mind. Try to avoid over-using notes and therefore losing eye contact with your audience. By learning the main ideas of your outline you will be able to deliver your speech without hesitation. Remember that learning your outline does not mean memorizing your speech.

2. Once you have learned your main points, sub-points and supporting material you should practice your speech aloud. While practicing you should also time the speech to see that you are within the limits allotted for the assignment.

3. Deliver your speech in a fresh and uncontrived manner. Meticulous preparation of content should not preclude naturalness in delivery. Diligent preparation and conversational delivery make an excellent combination.

Impromptu Delivery

When you are asked to speak on the spur of the moment, without advance notice or time for specific preparation, you are engaging in impromptu speaking. It has been remarked that much of our conversation is nothing more than a series of short, impromptu talks.

In facing an impromptu situation the speaker must quickly tie together all of his thoughts in a few seconds or minutes. The best preparation for impromptu speaking is being well informed and having practice in the prepared speaking situations. The speaker who knows how to prepare a speech when time is *not* a factor in preparation, will have little trouble in making the transition to the spur-of-the-moment occasion. Elsewhere in this volume we will examine the problems, principles and skills of impromptu speaking in an individualized manner.

ANALYZING THE AUDIENCE

As a high school student, didn't you go through the plight of trying to secure the family car for a date or for a shopping trip with the girls? You had a multitude of methods and devices you could use on your father as a means of gaining your desired end—the keys to the car. Arguments ranging from

"Dad, I'll wash the car" to "All my friends are driving" were used on those occasions. But when it came time for you to plead your case before your mother you most likely brought forth an entire new set of techniques. You discovered at an early age that what accomplished your purpose with Dad often failed with Mom. When talking to your parents on topics ranging from the car to staying out late at night you had to adjust your position, and hence your message, from person to person.

While you were considering your parents' attitude towards cars, driving, responsibility, etc., you were conducting an AUDIENCE ANALYSIS. And as you changed your message on each occasion you were using the material you gained from your analysis. AUDIENCE ANALYSIS means, in a very practical sense, finding out all you can about the people you are talking to or will be talking to. You discover what your receivers are like so that you can adapt your material directly to their needs, wants, experiences, and attitudes. Only by seeing things from their viewpoint can you deal directly with their predispositions. Remember that communication is a two-way process involving sender and receiver, and that the heart of communication is behavior change. In order to change someone's behavior we must, obviously, deal directly with him. The insurance man knows about his potential client before he prepares his "sales pitch." He must make direct contact if he is to be a successful communicator and accomplish his purpose.

The public speaker must also make an analysis of his audience if his speech is to be meaningful and not merely a verbal exercise. The speaker who presents his speech without considering his audience has very little chance of gaining support or being understood. Audience analysis enables a speaker to establish rapport with his listeners and to promote rapport amongst listeners. This he does by discovering some common denominators that exist in spite of individual and group differences. By understanding his audience the effective speaker can adapt his materials—and himself—to the people with whom he wants to communicate. Central to this idea, and to the entire process of communication, is the concept of identification. In his *Rhetoric of Motives,* Kenneth Burke suggests, "you persuade a man only insofar as you can talk his language by speech, gesture, tonality, order, image, attitude, idea, identifying your ways with his." What Burke is proposing is that successful speaking must necessarily ask the speaker to "talk the language" of those he hopes to influence. Audience analysis allows the speaker an opportunity to learn the language of his receivers so that he will be able to fuse his goals and purposes with theirs.

Your Listeners

Each particular audience, whether it be made up of one person or a large group, must be carefully analyzed to determine the best way of handling the subject for that distinct group. Your steps of analysis should include the following:

1. *Discover the age of your listeners.* You know from past experience that you talk differently to a group of junior high school students than to a class of college students. Even what you talk about is influenced by the age differences. As a speaker it is important for you to be sensitive to the problems that arise from age variations. Many times insight into age may also give insight into the past experiences of the audience. The depression, for example, may be a meaningful memory to an older person but only second-hand information to a younger individual. There are countless experimental studies that have revealed the effect age plays on interests, learning, opinion change and the like.

Admittedly, generalizations about different age groups are subject to many exceptions. Yet by and large, a group of old people will differ in attitude and experiences from a group of young people. This simple realization will greatly aid the speaker in selecting materials to accomplish his purpose.

2. *Discover the sex of your listeners.* Is it a mixed audience? The answer to this question may govern everything from your choice of subject to the examples you decide to place in your speech. Even though women have been "emancipated" in many areas the two sexes often live in two different worlds. A speech dealing with the offensive maneuvers of the Green Bay Packers

versus the Los Angeles Rams may well interest a group of college males but stands a good chance of boring a group of females.

3. *Try to find out the occupation of your listeners.* What a man does for a living is often a guide to his values, attitudes, and even his sense of humor. You know that a farmer may see things differently than a school teacher or a small shop owner. Ask yourself, is the occupation of my audience relevant to my topic?

4. *Discover the intelligence and educational level of your listeners.* In order for communication to take place it is necessary that the audience be able to understand what the speaker says. A speaker must be very careful not to overestimate or underestimate the intelligence of his listeners. In either case the cycle of communication can be broken if there is a lack of understanding. The speaker should remember that formal education as well as education acquired through practical experience will help determine what your audience thinks about and how they react.

5. *Try to discover to what social, professional, and religious groups your listeners belong.* We see ourselves and others in terms of the roles we play, and the groups to which we belong contribute to the making of these roles. Group membership suggests, in a general way, types of people, their points of view, interests and attitudes. It is apparent that such things as religious affiliation will influence our thinking on many topics. When you can learn the group membership of a large part of your audience you have gained a valuable clue to listeners' attitudes and wants.

In addition to exploring the attitudes of your listeners, it is also useful to ask a number of other questions once you have established a profile of your audience. (1) What does the audience already know about me? (2) What is the audience's attitude toward me? (3) What does the audience's know about the subject? (4) What is the audience opinion of my subject? (5) What brings the audience together? The answer to each of these questions will make possible a more complete understanding of the entire speaking situation.

Your Speaking Occasion

We have already established the importance of knowing your audience as a means of selecting, preparing, adapting and adjusting your speech so that it will accomplish your preconceived purpose. The speaking occasion also demands a careful analysis. Indeed, where you deliver your speech plays a prominent role in the entire communication process. A famous American humorist once observed that he could never speak in jest in a church chapel.

A speaker's analysis of the occasion should involve the following considerations:

1. *What kind of occasion will it be?* This question is relevant because it affects the tone and purpose of the meeting, and hence the speech itself. Your initial concern should therefore be to discover why the meeting is being held. Have the people gathered only to hear your speech or do they meet on a regular basis? The speaker should also know whether the procedure will be ritualistic, parliamentary, formal, or informal. Finally, questions pertaining to the location of the meeting and the time of day should be investigated. All of these factors will have an influence on the speech.

2. *What will the physical surroundings be like?* The physical setting in which the speech is delivered often contributes considerably to the success or failure of the speaker's attempt to get his message across. The speaker should consider factors related to whether or not the speech is delivered indoors or outside, the acoustics of the room or hall, the presence or absence of a public address system, the seating arrangements, lighting arrangements, and any outside distractions and noises. All of these factors will govern, to some degree, the mood and attention span of the audience.

3. *What will precede and follow the speech?* The speaker should know whether or not his speech comes before or after dinner, whether other speakers will precede him, and whether his is part of a series of speeches. His "spot" on the program will influence his material.

4. *Are there any rules, rituals, and customs associated with the gathering?* The customs of the meeting might well have

a control over the speaker's dress, delivery, language and choice of subject.

EMPATHY

During the last section of this chapter we have endeavored to substantiate the concept that to be an effective communicator one must take into account the person or persons who are to receive the message. The speaker is but one half of the communication process; the audience is the second half. Being able to understand the audience is, in a real sense, being able to see things as the audience sees them. Once you are able to see and to feel as the audience does, you are in a position to put into words those ideas that will elicit maximum agreement and understanding.

All human communication, to one degree or another, demands that the sender of a message make some predictions about how people will respond to that message. We can say that all of us carry around in our mind images of other people, and take these images into account whenever we speak. We noted earlier that your image of your mother and father influenced what you said and how you said it. The successful communicator is one who is accurate in his prediction and fully understands the person to whom he is talking. When we make predictions we are assuming we have skill in what the psychologist calls EMPATHY—the process of projecting ourselves into other peoples' personalities. By trying to place ourselves in the shoes of the receiver we are developing empathy. Audience analysis is but one means of developing empathy. By analyzing your audience, finding out their attitudes, desires, backgrounds, interests and goals, you are constructing a picture of them that will enable you to make predictions. It is only by empathy—the sharing of another's personality—that one can hope to send messages that are meaningful and real.

The audience also experiences a kind of empathy during the speaking situation. As the speaker delivers his talk the audience is "feeling" (sharing) the experiences along with him. For example, when the speaker appears nervous and tense the audience also feels uncomfortable and strained. When the speaker can manifest sincere enthusiasm the audience will also experience a similar sensation. The speaker should therefore be aware of this mutual rapport, and his appearance and actions should attempt to make the audience feel at ease.

FEEDBACK

By reviewing some earlier principles we will be in a position to suggest still another vital concept of communication. You will recall the precept that the goal of all communication is the securing of a predetermined response and that the speaker should analyze his audience so that he will be able to communicate directly with them and thus induce the response. By knowing the attitudes and needs of an audience the speaker makes predictions concerning how they will respond to his message. We noted in the first chapter that a trained speaker looks directly at his listeners so that they will feel he is interested in them, and we observed that the speaker should look at his audience as a means of ascertaining the group's reaction to what he says. It is this final point, the concept of taking stock of your audience's reactions, that warrants further discussion.

The term FEEDBACK applies directly to (1) the reactions that you try to obtain from your listeners and (2) your efforts in adapting yourself to these perceived reactions. The term was originally used only in the literature of engineering and cybernetics to designate the feeding back of information to the machine so that the machine could adjust itself to changing conditions. A thermostat is an example of a device that employs the principles of feedback. As information related to the original message (heat) is fed back into the machine there is an act performed that enables the machine to readjust—to shut off the heater when the air is hot and to turn it on when the air is cold. The source is having to make adjustments because of the information it is receiving.

Feedback in human communication is really nothing more than perceiving how the audience is reacting to the messages you send. The speaker, by seeing how the audience reacts, can adjust and adapt his message in much the same way employed by the thermostatically-controlled furnace. Feedback, in this instance, is providing the speaker with essential information concerning his success in accomplishing his objectives. In so doing, feedback controls future messages. Whether the speaker is talking to one or one-hundred, he has the two-fold task of (1) observing and interpreting audience reactions and (2) readjusting his next message in light of his observations and interpretations. It isn't enough for the speaker simply to think about what he is saying. This thinking must be carried on in terms of what he perceives to be the audience's reaction. The question, "Am I being understood?" should consistently be running through his mind. He should try to estimate the probable degree of attention and interest he is creating. By using feedback he can note if the audience is restless or at ease. Are they yawning, drawing pictures or whispering? All of these reactions might well indicate a lack of interest. The discriminating speaker, by using the principles of feedback, may even gather clues as to whether or not the audience agrees with him or objects to what he is saying. Frowns, headnodding, smiles and other facial expressions may very well indicate the degree of conviction being produced in the listeners.

In everyday conversation what we say at any given moment generally depends on what others have said in response to our previous remarks. The same rule applies to public speaking. The audience will offer the speaker an assortment of clues, and it is his responsibility to use this information. He should, not hesitate to change his "planned" speech and employ some device to retrieve the wandering attention of an audience. For example, if you were attempting to explain the musical concept of "counterpoint," and you noted, through feedback, that some members of your audience were obviously not following your explanation, you might decide to insert a clarifying example or illustration. The effective speaker is ever ready to modify his message and his delivery if the situation warrants such adjustments.

An awareness and utilization of feedback increases one's communication effectiveness in all situations—both public and private. Being able to observe the reactions of others is one of the characteristics of a person who is "sensitive" to the urgency of understanding and being understood.

SUMMARY

Communication normally takes place because the speaker wants to achieve some preconceived purpose. Thus the purpose must be clear in his mind. The public speaker will usually be preparing and giving speeches that fall into three general speech purposes — to INFORM, to PERSUADE, and to ENTERTAIN. In addition to selecting a general purpose the speaker must formulate a specific purpose which describes the immediate and exact nature of the response wanted from the audience.

The speaker may encounter situations that make it necessary for him to furnish a title for his speech. In those cases it is important to remember that a good title is brief, appropriate, interesting, and suggests the nature of the purpose.

In deciding on a method of preparation and delivery the speaker can utilize any one of the following procedures: (1) speaking from a manuscript, (2) speaking from memory, (3) extemporaneous speaking, and (4) impromptu speaking. The extemporaneous method is the one most recommended for the beginning speaker.

In order to adapt his purpose to a specific audience the speaker should analyze his audience. He can gain valuable insight into the listeners' needs, wants, attitudes and experiences by discovering their age, sex, occupation, intelligence and education, and social, professional and religious affiliations.

By implementing the material gathered through an analysis of the audience and occasion the speaker can use empathy— the projecting of himself into the personalities of his listeners. Knowing what his listeners are like enables him to "speak their language."

By using feedback, the speaker continues his analysis of the audience even during the speech. By seeing the reactions brought about by his message, the speaker is able to change and alter his remarks to fit the immediate and real situation that confronts him.

SUGGESTED READINGS

JANE BLANKENSHIP, *Public Speaking: A Rhetorical Perspective*, (Englewood Cliffs, N. J.: Prentice-Hall, 1966). Chapter 3.

DONALD C. BRYANT and KARL WALLACE, *Fundamentals of Public Speaking*, (New York: Appleton-Century-Crofts, 1960). Chapters 18 and 19.

E. C. BUEHLER and WIL A. LINKUGEL, *Speech: A First Course*, (New York: Harper and Brothers, 1962). Chapter 5.

KENNETH BURKE, *A Rhetoric of Motives*, (New York: Prentice Hall, Inc., 1950).

GLEN R. CAPP, *How to Communicate Orally*, (Englewood Cliffs, N. J.: Prentice-Hall, Inc., 1961). Chapter 4.

HERBERT L. CARSON, *Steps in Successful Speaking*, (Princeton, N. J.: D. Van Nostrand Co., Inc., 1967). Part II.

JON EISENSON, J. JEFFREY AUER, and JOHN V. IRWIN, *The Psychology of Communication*, (New York: Appleton-Century-Crofts, 1963). Chapter 16.

HUBER W. ELLINGSWORTH, and THEODORE CLEVENGER, JR., *Speech and Social Action*. (Englewood Cliffs, N. J.: Prentice-Hall, 1967). Chapters 5 and 6.

JAMES H. HENNING, *Improving Oral Communication*, (New York: McGraw-Hill Book Company, 1966). Chapter 2.

JAMES H. MCBURNEY, and ERNEST J. WRAGE, *The Art of Good Speech*, (Englewood Cliffs, N. J.: Prentice-Hall, Inc., 1953). Chapter 11.

ELWOOD MURRAY, *The Speech Personality*, (New York: Lippincott, 1937).

KEITH R. ST. ONGE, *Creative Speech*, (Belmont, Calif.: Wadsworth, 1964). Chapter 2.

LEE O. THAYER, *Administrative Communication*, (Homewood, Illinois: Richard D. Irwin, Inc., 1961). Chapter 2.

CARL H. WEAVER, *Speaking in Public*, (New York: American Book Company, 1966). Chapter 17.

LISTENING

EVALUATION AND CRITICISM

Inherent in our definition and explanation of communication is the concept that speech is a two-way process. Speaking and listening are the two indispensable ingredients of communication; there can be no effective speech without someone to listen. If our discussion of oral communication is to have real meaning, then, we must give a proper share of attention to listening.

Listening plays a vital and essential role in our individual lives and, indeed, in our civilization. Much of what we know about the past has come to us through listening. The small child learns much about his new world through listening, for it is his first means of acquiring information and ideas about his environment. As adults we use listening more than any other communication skill. The time we spend in listening far exceeds the time we spend in reading, writing, or speaking. It has been estimated that we spend 40 to 50 per cent of our total communication time engaged in listening. One of the authors of this text conducted a research project which led to the conclusion that we may be spending more than one-third of our waking hours listening. Stop in the middle of what you are doing a few times during the day and you will soon discover that the statistics concerning listening are quite valid. We listen at home, on the job, at school and at play.

But what kind of listeners are we? There is sufficient evidence to support the generalization that people, as a whole, are poor listeners. Two separate studies concluded that a large percentage of those tested could not locate a central idea after listening to exposition which had been designed for clarity and simplicity. Other results point to the generalization that listeners are able to comprehend only a small percentage of what they hear. Perhaps the best proof for the assertion that people are poor listeners can be found by some serious self-introspection on the part of all of us. Many of the most common communication breakdowns can indeed be assigned to faulty listening. Too many of us have been conditioned to believe that if we don't understand something it is the fault of the speaker.

Research into the listening habits of students also reveals some alarming results. Ask yourself how well you rank in regard to the six common weaknesses uncovered by researchers:

1. People tend to stop listening when the material is uninteresting. The findings show that most of us pay attention only to that material we "like" listening to.

2. People tend to be influenced more by the dramatic elements of a message than by logical elements.

3. Most people have a short listening span.

4. Most listeners have a difficult time separating the essential from the non-essential.

5. Listeners are influenced more by the speaker's voice than by the "truth" of his message.

6. People tend to believe what they hear in broadcast speeches. Their assumption seems to be that if a speaker is on radio or television, he must be important and his ideas therefore merit belief.

Substituting these common faults with good listening habits can produce important benefits. Good listening enables you to add to your storehouse of information, to update and revise your collection of facts, skills, attitudes, and beliefs. It adds depth and dimension to even the simplest daily experiences. You will find yourself noticing and appreciating things of which you had previously been unaware. This sharpened awareness is also good protection against the devices and techniques of the unethical and sophistic speaker. It should also be noted that good listening is not the same thing as paying attention. It is far more complicated and involved. Finally, good listening helps to improve your speaking. By listening carefully to the speeches of others you will be able to select those characteristics of content and delivery which ought to be emulated and those which should be avoided.

You will discover that most of the time spent in speech class is spent in listening to student speeches and to remarks of the instructor. In fact, you will probably listen to over one hundred speeches in your class while delivering only five or six. Take full advantage of this listening time to sharpen your perception and you will be a better speaker as well as a better listener for the experience.

HOW WE LISTEN

The act of listening consists of two component activities— the physical operation of a sense organ and an accompanying mental process. Some authorities distinguish *hearing* from *listening*, maintaining that when we hear, we perceive sounds only, but when we listen this hearing is accompanied by a deliberate and purposeful act of the mind. To listen means to get meaning from that which is heard. This distinction has merit in that it cautions us that attention to a speaker's voice is no guarantee of efficient listening.

The way in which we listen is of course dependent upon our reason for listening. For most communication situations there appear to be the following levels of listening:

1. Listening to answer a definite question.
2. Listening to a question with the intention of answering it.
3. Listening to form an opinion on a controversial question.
4. Listening for news.
5. Listening to an argument in order to answer it.
6. Listening to directions which one expects to follow.
7. Listening for unspecified information on a topic in which one is interested.

BARRIERS TO EFFECTIVE LISTENING

If the communication process was not such a complex phenomenon we would not have cause to discuss the barriers to listening. However, because the human mind is such a complicated instrument and not subject to simple stimulus-response relationships, there are many variables that exert themselves whenever we try to listen.

Physical Conditions as a Barrier

As a listener you will experience physical barriers over which you have no control and those over which you will be able to exercise some regulation. Distracting sounds, poor acoustics, and uncomfortable seating arrangements may usually be classified as distractions which you can't manipulate, although there are times when you can move your seat or close a window. The most effective device for surmounting most physical barriers is *concentration*, the core of all good listening.

The real danger of physical barriers is that the listener may use the barrier (distraction) as an excuse for "tuning the speaker out." We all know from experience that we can yield to any distraction quite easily, and thus make this distraction the main focus of our attention. The conscientious listener and the sincere speaker are aware of the problems caused by physical barriers, and both work diligently to overcome these obstructions to listening.

Speaking-Thinking Rate as a Barrier

It is estimated that we speak an average of 125 to 150 words per minute. Our mind, however, is able to cope with approximately 400 words per minute. This means that the mind has a great deal of "idle" time. This excess time forms one of the major barriers to proficient listening. In most instances the time is spent in wandering away from the task of critical and careful listening. It is during this "free time" that many listeners surrender to external distractions. The listening-thinking gap is often used for mental excursions ranging from daydreaming to thinking about the speaker's necktie. It would be far more beneficial to both sender and receiver if this time were spent analyzing the message.

Status and Role as a Barrier

Experimental evidence indicates that your impression of a person's status will determine, to a large degree, what you learn from him and what influence he will have over your attitudes. From your own experience you have seen how your regard for the speaker influences what you actually hear. Status relationships between speaker and listener, as well as the various roles they both play, frequently determine the success or failure of the communication act.

We also know from research that when we respect someone we tend to listen more attentively. Unfortunately, we may become overly-concerned with the speaker as a person and neglect to think critically about what he is saying. This barrier applies both to speakers for whom we have a high regard as well as to those for whom we have a lower regard. The good listener must recognize prestige, role and status as factors present in all communication and he must not let them prevent maximum comprehension and evaluation of what is being said.

Lack of Common Experiences as a Barrier

A barrier in listening can occur when speaker and listener are far apart in their backgrounds and in their current living environments. It is difficult to understand what is being said if you have not experienced, either directly or indirectly, the concepts being discussed. A college graduate, born and raised in a large eastern city, may well have a difficult time understanding and experiencing the messages and ideas of a farmer who has spent his entire life in a small rural community. A true meeting of the minds is hampered when speaker and listener have lived in two separate worlds.

Preconceived Attitudes as a Barrier

When we listen we also make abundant use of our prejudices and our personal beliefs. These attitudes are usually deepseated and developed over a long period of time, and it is therefore not always easy to create a posture of open-mindedness. A Democrat listening to a Republican speaker will probably not give him a fair hearing because of preconceived attitudes he holds about the characteristics of Republicanism. But if one is to break down the barrier of preconceived attitudes he must try to exert some command over his emotions and his initial responses. He must try to hold off judgement until he has *listened*—listened completely and objectively to what was said.

Being Overly Engrossed with "Self" as a Barrier

Our natural tendency to think about ourselves can be a barrier to effective listening. We all know from experience that while a speaker is talking we can engage in another conversation with the "little fellow who lives in our skull." Many of us will find ourselves thinking about the coming weekend at the same instant the speaker before us is discussing collective bargaining in the United States. Daydreaming is usually nothing more than being engrossed in one's self to the degree that all other sources of information are blocked out. Being overly concerned with one's self impedes the ability to gain anything concrete from the communication situation.

It is important to remember that these barriers can destroy the critical link between speaker and listener. In communication we receive word-symbols representing someone else's message and we attempt to extract from them the meaning intended by the sender. In speaking we cannot go back and re-listen as we can go back and re-read; so the word-symbol relationship must be free from barriers whenever possible.

IMPROVING YOUR LISTENING

Listening is one of the communication skills that can be improved with serious practice and training. A large number of research projects, in particular those conducted by Ralph Nichols of the University of Minnesota, demonstrate that listening ability can be enriched if the individual desires such enrichment. Your speech class offers an arena for just such practice and training.

Be Motivated to Listen

Probably the most important step you can take in becoming a better listener is to resolve that *you will listen* more efficiently. This simple commitment will give you a sound new attitude about listening, and improvement will be noticeable at once. What we suggest is quite transparent—*want to listen.*

Efficient listening begins with motivation. Researchers in the area of listening have concluded that if one is motivated to listen, he will be a more alert and active receiver. The material will be more meaningful if you believe it affects you personally. If you have motives for listening, you will not allow yourself to be easily distracted. What prompts you to listen might be something as pragmatic as making a sale if you listen carefully to what your customer is saying or as abstract as listening because you "owe it to the speaker." In either case, if you are motivated, you will discover that you can not be easily distracted.

Although motivation, in itself, is not enough to overcome all problems in listening, it is the first prerequisite to becoming a good listener. In short, the good listener brings the following attitudes to the listening situation: (1) he wants to listen, (2) he finds a personal reason for listening, and (3) he is willing to do his part in the listening situation.

Be Prepared to Listen

An effective listener begins to think about listening even before the speaker sends his first message by keeping himself informed on topics that he may have occasion to judge and evaluate.

For specific listening experiences he prepares himself in four ways:

1. He tries to learn all he can about the subject, speaker and situation. This knowledge, much like an audience analysis, will help the listener understand and appraise what the speaker will say. It will also aid him in comprehending and overcoming the problems of word-symbol relationships.

2. He tries to minimize physical barriers by placing himself in a position where he can easily see and hear the speaker.

3. He tries to eliminate all those distractions in his environment which might call attention away from the speaker. For

example, he leaves the school newspaper outside the classroom, anticipating that it might later become a distraction.

4. He is ready to take notes when appropriate. Having to stop and look for paper and pencil during the talk may force the listener to miss key points.

Be Objective

You can improve your listening immeasurably by maintaining an attitude of objectivity as you listen to what is being discussed. If you approach a communication situation with an open mind and a spirit of inquiry, you stand to gain far more than the listener who says, "Here comes another dull talk; I've heard this topic discussed over and over, and I still feel the same way."

Attend critically to each of the speaker's words, but do not make judgements until points are fully developed. Be alert for items that are implausible and misleading; but be aware of the larger principle the speaker is developing. Let the speaker explain and summarize all his main points before you draw final conclusions.

We cease to be objective listeners when we allow our emotions and our prejudices to control our understanding. As we listen to speakers who profess views alien to our own, we sometimes fail to hear them out because our feelings are so deeply involved. Our natural tendency is to start composing a rebuttal of the opposing ideas and thinking of further arguments. Our emotions are getting in the way of what is actually being said. Admittedly, it is difficult to control our emotions and our preconceived attitudes, but conscious effort to declare a truce with bias will aid our over-all comprehension of what is being expressed.

Be Alert to All Clues

In listening it is important to look for the speaker's *main* ideas. This must be a conscious and diligent search, for we cannot expect every speaker to underline his main point or stop and say, "What follows is my central thesis."

Be watchful for all specific clues to meaning as contained in the elements of the speaking situation. The setting, the staging of the event, and the program notes can give insight into what will be said. The speaker's inflection, rate, emphasis, voice quality, and bodily actions can often offer clues to the meaning of what is being said and what the speaker feels is most important.

Clues naturally abound in the content and arrangement of the material. The vigilant listener makes note of the speaker's use of partitions, enumerations, transitions, topic sentences, and internal and final summaries. Clues common to writing, such as bold type, italics and quotation marks, are replaced with clues of voice, body, material and arrangement.

Make Use of the Thinking-Speaking Time Difference

As noted earlier, evidence indicates that we normally think at a pace about three times faster than our speaking pace. A good listener uses this time to think about what the speaker is saying. He can ask himself, "How does this item relate to the speaker's main purpose? How does this main point support that purpose?" An alert listener can make this time gap work for him instead of against him. By concentrating on what is being said, instead of worrying or mentally arguing with the speaker, the listener puts the time difference to efficient use. This extra time can also be used to take notes when the situation warrants such action. Finally, the free time can always be used to summarize mentally and review what the speaker has said.

Avoid the "Mystery of Words" Fallacy

A good listener is always aware of the fact that the words being used by the speaker may not accurately represent what the speaker thinks or feels. The person talking is using words to represent an idea or a feeling; *the word is not the idea or feeling but rather an abstract symbol standing for what the speaker really means.* The trained listener tries to go beyond the words he hears. He is concerned with the speaker's motives and purposes. Finding out *why* someone is talking can often yield information far more valuable than that gained from the words themselves.

Empathy provides another way of avoiding the "mystery of words" fallacy. If you can see the problem (issue) the way the speaker sees it, the chances of reaching a mutual frame of reference will be greatly enhanced. In essence, you must ask yourself if the words being used by the speaker really represent his *true* feelings and ideas.

Practice Listening

Proficiency in any skill usually is the result of a great deal of conscientious effort. *You should therefore practice listening.* The poor listener avoids difficult listening situations and evades dull material. A case in point might be a college lecture on some highly abstract concept which defies the application of interest devices by even the most skillful speaker. In such cases the listener has to work along with the speaker at gaining meaning. It is a great temptation to stop listening when listening requires effort. Because of this the weak listener never improves. Force yourself to practice; make yourself listen to music, speeches, and conversations that seem to hold no *obvious* interest value.

LISTENING TO SPEECHES

The act of receiving oral language involves three things: (1) the recall or deduction of meanings from each spoken word-symbol, (2) the comprehension of ideas presented by different combinations of these word-symbols, and (3) the use of the ideas presented to build understanding by adding to, modifying, or rejecting previous learning. We must perceive, comprehend and finally use or reject what the speaker says.

We are constantly being besieged with requests to vote, give, buy, feel, and think in one way or another. A poor listener is easy prey for the sophist, huckster, shyster and propagandist. Our major defenses against those who choose to influence and control our behavior are critical thinking and captious evaluation. Both of these skills can be learned, and your speech class, by allowing you an opportunity to hear over a hundred speeches, is an excellent place to cultivate your listening ability.

As a speech critic, both in class and out, you have a responsibility to listen attentively if you are to judge and evaluate, and possibly accept or reject what is being said.

Speech Criticism

Speech criticism in class usually involves pointing out praise-worthy qualities in the speech, weaknesses in the speech, and offering suggestions for improvement. Since constructive criticism is contingent upon critical listening, we should examine some of the attributes of the critical listener.

The critical listener seeks to distinguish the issue from the man. We can sometimes become so impressed with a speaker's personality, with his voice, with his "image," that we neglect to evaluate what he is saying. The critical listener separates what the speaker says from what the speaker is.

The critical listener is aware of the problems inherent in our language and our use of words. He is aware of the fact that words are only symbols standing for things—they are not the things themselves. He recognizes the loaded word and the ambiguous word. He learns to be careful of words such as "un-American," "freedom," "liberalism," "socialism," or "extremism." He knows that words have real meaning only if they represent something in reality. He recognizes that one word may have many uses, and he tries to interpret the speaker's meaning in light of this variety of uses.

The critical listener applies the tests of evidence and reasoning. He is familiar with the propaganda techniques we have discussed, and is able to isolate the half-truth, name-calling and the other devices.

The critical listener detects the substitution of generalities for specifics—of glibness for sincerity. He demands dates, names, numbers, places. He knows that the speaker who omits key information is often the same person who relies on innuendoes and who exaggerates some points out of proportion to their importance while understating other more fundamental points (a favorite device of Adolph Hitler).

The critical listener applies the tests of evidence and reasoning (to be discussed in Chapter V) to the material presented by the speaker. He is concerned with the validity and reliability of illustrations, examples, statistics, testimony, and analogies. By checking the authenticity of the facts presented and the probability that the facts mean what they are said to mean, he is able to make more accurate judgements.

The critical listener questions the relevance of the material offered by the speaker. He knows that material may meet all the tests of reliability and validity and yet be irrelevant to the point under discussion. "So what?" or "What is the point?" are the critical listener's inevitable questions.

Evaluating Speeches

At the end of most classroom speeches you will have an opportunity to present an informal critique, either oral or written. As you evaluate the speeches of others try to implement the broad principles discussed by your instructor and by this text. The following items are designed to serve as a guide for your assignments in speech evaluation:

1. Has the speaker made an attempt to be objective and fair to himself, the audience, and the subject? Did the speaker seem to care about communicating, or was he simply going through the motions of fulfilling an assignment? Or was he simply enjoying "holding the floor?"

2. Did the speaker have a worthwhile purpose? Was the purpose clear? Was it easy to follow and logically developed?

3. Did the speaker know his subject? Did he seem to be prepared both in terms of research and in terms of oral practice?

4. Was there evidence that the speaker had analyzed his audience? Were such factors as the audience's age, sex, education, and attitudes taken into consideration? Did the speaker indicate that the speech was being directed at the classroom audience or at some hypothetical audience?

5. Was the speech structurally sound? Did the subdivisions, both major and minor, relate to and support the main ideas? Were the transitions between ideas clear?

6. Did the speaker utilize language meaningfully? Did he employ words or phrases that were clear and adequately defined? Did he make effective use of imagery and word pictures? Did he avoid cliches, slang, poor grammar? Was his usage appropriate to the audience, the occasion, the subject?

7. Did the speaker utilize factors of attention and interest in both the content and delivery of the speech?

8. Did the speaker's illustrations, examples, statistics, testimony and analogies meet the tests of evidence? Was enough evidence employed to support each point?

9. How effectively did the speaker employ visual aspects of delivery? Did he maintain good eye contact? Did he have good posture? Were his gestures and movements skillfully executed? Did he have animated facial expressions?

10. How effectively did he employ his voice? Was there sufficient variety of rate, pitch, loudness? Was his enunciation clear and his pronunciation correct?

11. What was the total impression left by the speech?

12. How successfully did the speaker fulfill the demands of the specific speech assignment?

These are by no means the only categories for evaluation. Doubtless you will discover others as you gain experience in listening to various types of speeches.

One further suggestion. Listen carefully to your classmates as they evaluate other speeches and speakers. You may very well find that your own speaking may profit from remarks directed to other speakers.

SUMMARY

Listening is one of our most important communication skills. Effective listening is an active process that demands conscientious effort on the part of the listener. Virtually everyone can improve his listening ability by simply becoming aware of some of the problems of listening and their remedies.

The listener who is sincere about improvement should be alert to the major barriers to effective listening: physical conditions, speaking-thinking rate, status and role relationships, lack of common experiences, preconceived attitudes, and being overly engrossed with "self."

Overcoming these, and other problems of listening, can be aided if the listener will:

1. Get mentally prepared to listen.
2. Find or create a reason for listening.
3. Be physically set to listen.
4. Start listening at the first sentence.

5. Develop a positive attitude toward the speaker and his message.
6. Be objective and try not to let his prejudices interfere.
7. Not yield to distractions.
8. Follow the speaker's purpose.
9. Be critical, not a "sponge."
10. Ask questions of himself and review during the speech.
11. Be aware of the word-mystery fallacy; look beyond the words.
12. Be alert to non-verbal clues.
13. Continue to think about, use, and evaluate what he has heard.
14. Practice listening.

SUGGESTED READINGS

EDWIN BLACK, *Rhetorical Criticism: A Study in Method*, (New York: The Macmillan Company, 1965).

JANE BLANKENSHIP, *Public Speaking: A Rhetorical Perspective*, (Englewood Cliffs, N. J.: Prentice-Hall, 1966). Chapter 10.

ROBERT CATHCART, *Post Communication: Critical Analysis and Evaluation*, (New York: Bobbs-Merrill Company, Inc., 1966).

Education, LXXV, (January, 1955). This entire issue is devoted to listening.

PAUL W. KELLER, "Major Findings in Listening in the Past Ten Years," *The Journal of Communication*, X, (March, 1960), 29-38.

RALPH G. NICHOLS and THOMAS R. LEWIS, *Listening and Speaking*, (Dubuque, Iowa: Wm. C. Brown Co., Inc., 1965).

RALPH G. NICHOLS and LEONARD A. STEVENS, *Are You Listening?*, (New York: McGraw-Hill, 1957).

CARL R. ROGERS, and R. J. ROETHLISBERGER, "Barriers and Gateways to Communication" *Harvard Business Review*, XXX, No. 4, (July-August, 1952).

LESTER THONSSEN, and A. CRAIG BAIRD, *Speech Criticism: The Development of Standards for Rhetorical Appraisal*, (New York: Ronald Press, 1948).

WILLIAM H. WHYTE, JR., *Is Anybody Listening?*, (New York: Simon and Schuster, Inc., 1952).

SOUND AND ACTION

DELIVERING THE MESSAGE

To possess ideas worth communicating, to have them arranged in a meaningful sequence, and to have them worded accurately, interestingly and appropriately is not enough for effective oral communication. Countless worthwhile ideas probably go unheeded because they are delivered ineptly (or are not delivered at all), and countless others are misinterpreted because of flaws in their delivery.

We do not wish to suggest that the speaker's delivery is something apart from his message. In reality, the speaker's delivery is *part* of his message. The listener derives meaning from the non-verbal elements of the message (the auditory and visual stimuli emanating from the speaker) that help him to interpret the verbal elements of the message. Imperfections in communication may result when the non-verbal elements are not supportive of the verbal elements—the speaker's words tell you one thing while his voice and actions tell you something quite apart. Which set of elements are you going to believe?

The purpose of this chapter will be to suggest principles which may assist you in bringing the non-verbal means of communication into alignment with the verbal. First, we will discuss the role of the visual elements—your appearance and your bodily actions—and then we will examine the vocal elements.

MOVEMENT

In order to appreciate the role and importance of bodily action in communication, we should be aware of these two facts about the nature of movement: (1) movement is a conveyor of meaning, and (2) movement is a factor of attention.

Movement and Meaning

To watch a television program with the audio turned down is to witness the power of movement to communicate meaning. We can see at times that no dialogue is taking place—that the meaning is being communicated solely through actions. The heroine stamps her foot in anger over a broken dish, the hero raises an amused eyebrow. No dialogue is necessary to complete the message. At other times the movement suggests only the speaker's attitude or emotional state. We need the dialogue to complete the meaning. We know the speaker is angry, but we don't know what he is angry about. So we turn up the sound to learn that he is grousing about an impending visit from his mother-in-law. Or perhaps the speaker's movements are quite unrelated to what he is saying at the moment. Finally, the speaker's movements may actually transmit a meaning which is contradictory to the meaning being transmitted by his words. The obviously tired and bored announcer mouthing extravagant words of praise for a product is a common case in point. He is going through the motions of enthusiasm but there is a flaccidity about his actions that tell us he is pretending.

Movement and Attention

If you were to glance up from this page for a few moments, the chances are that your eyes would rove idly around the room, not resting on anything in particular, until there was movement of some sort. Perhaps an automobile would go past your window or a curtain would stir in the breeze. Instantly your eyes would fasten on the moving object and would linger there until some more powerful stimulus drew them away. *Movement draws attention.*

There are many applications of this factor of attention in various media of communication. A motion picture will attract our attention more quickly than a still picture. A still picture that *depicts action* will attract our attention more quickly than one which depicts a static situation. Similarly, a flashing neon sign attracts us more quickly than a steadily glowing sign. The movement causes us to keep our eyes, and thus our attention, on the object.

The principle of movement and attention in the mass media also applies to public speaking. Given this power to intensify audience attention through bodily action, we are unwise not to employ it. Yet we will root ourselves in one spot, usually behind a lectern, and remain there for the duration of the speech. We will grip the lectern or thrust our hands in our pockets or otherwise immobilize them so that they can't be used for meaningful gestures. If we are to compete successfully with all of the other stimuli that are fighting to gain the audience's attention, then we must utilize those means that help us to become the dominant stimulus. Movement is one of those means.

Now let us add an important qualification to our observations about the power of movement to gain and hold attention. Movements both graceful and awkward, appropriate and inappropriate, helpful and distracting, draw our attention. So movement can be an asset or a liability. It will be an asset only if it directs the audience's attention ultimately to the verbal message being communicated.

The movement must enhance or augment the verbal message. Its effect should be essentially subliminal. Once we begin to notice the speaker's actions rather than his words then communication of ideas is interrupted.

Posture

If we may agree that meaningful bodily action is desirable in speaking, then we should adopt a stance or posture which encourages, or at least does not inhibit, easy, spontaneous action.

Perhaps we can determine the characteristics of such a stance if we look first at some undesirable postures. The most common of these are called variously "the coed slouch" or "debutante slouch," the "Colossus of Rhodes" or "drill sergeant," and the "Attention!" or "heels together" stance. The "coed slouch" or "debutante slouch," is characterized by having most of the weight on one leg, while the other leg relaxes in a casual position, bent at the knee. This stance tends to inhibit movement because we must first return to a position of equilibrium before we move to right or left, to front or rear. So we take the course of least resistance and remain in the slouch! This posture not only inhibits movement, but conveys an impression of lethargy or apathy. What we are saying may be forceful or moving but our posture is sending the audience a contradictory signal.

"The Colossus of Rhodes" or "drill sergeant" requires planting the feet widely apart as though guarding an entrance to the room or preparing to issue orders to the troops. This stance inhibits movement, because, like the "coed slouch," it requires us to bring our feet closer together before we initiate movement to another spot on the platform. The posture itself suggests that the speaker's attitude is domineering, officious, intractable. Imagine trying to deliver a conciliatory message while standing in a posture that shouts defiance!

The "Attention!" or "heels together" posture describes the speaker who is stiffly erect with his feet very close together. This posture encourages movement of the wrong kind. After a few moments in this imbalanced posture we tend to sway from side to side or rock back and forth on our heels in a manner quite distracting to the audience. The posture itself suggests that the speaker is very tense and nervous.

To be sure, there may be times when we will *temporarily* adopt these postures with impunity because they happen to fit most comfortably with the ideas we are expressing at the moment. Perhaps leaning on the lectern or sitting on the edge of the table will actually enhance the communication of a given idea or attitude. But as general "working" postures they should be avoided because they inhibit meaningful, spontaneous bodily action, and they may well send misleading signals to the audience.

The posture which seems to facilitate spontaneous bodily actions and which communicates an impression of ease and alertness is simply that one which has these characteristics: the weight is distributed evenly on both legs, the feet are placed a comfortable distance apart, perhaps six to ten inches, the arms are allowed to hang comfortably at the sides, and the shoulders are held straight, (but not rigidly so). Some speakers maintain that you can acquire this posture by imagining that your head is being held erect by a puppeteer's string. From this starting position we will find it much easier to move when we feel so compelled.

Movement on the Platform

Movement from one place to another on the platform is generally motivated either by (1) a transition in ideas or by (2) a desire to make an idea more emphatic. Lateral movements (to the speaker's right or left) are useful in signaling a change from one point in the speech to the following point. Picture how such a lateral movement would readily accompany this statement: "So much for the economic consequences. Now what about the political consequences?"

The actual distance we will cover in a transitional movement will, of course, depend on such things as how long it takes us to deliver the transitional statement, the physical dimensions of the platform, the presence or absence of a microphone.

A movement toward the audience is generally associated with our desire to make an idea emphatic. "Now listen to this," says one person, *leaning toward* his listener in a conversation. The same principle operates in the public speaking situation except that the movement may be more pronounced; instead of leaning toward the listeners, we may actually take a step or two toward them.

We have earlier observed that the wrong kind of movement can measurably reduce a speech's effectiveness. The authors recall one speaker who was called "Toro" by his classmates because of his propensity to paw the floor with his feet while speaking. The pencil tapper and the sleeve tugger also come to mind. It is probably better to have no movement at all than to have such distracting movements. These movements are, of course, manifestations of nervous tension seeking release. The best way to avoid the build-up of this tension is to employ the meaningful movements we have discussed, thus affording the tension a constructive outlet.

GESTURE

"Tie his hands behind his back and he can't talk!" How often we have heard this pointed reminder of the importance of gestures to the communicative attempts of some persons. Indeed, many persons are able to use gestures as substitutes for the spoken word. While we have no wish to propound a theory of communication based on gesture alone, we do wish to remind you of the power of gestural activity to heighten attention and to intensify the meaning conveyed by the spoken word. Next time you are engaged in a communication act stop and notice the impact of non-verbal communication.

Perhaps no other aspect of visual communication bothers the beginning speaker as much as gesturing. "But it doesn't feel natural!" is a lament that every speech teacher hears when he asks a student to employ gestural activity. Yet that same student, in a conversation out in the hall, probably utilizes scores of gestures and isn't even aware that he's doing so. Why does he "freeze up" in front of an audience? Why does the act of gesturing feel "unnatural?"

Most of us acquire a number of inhibitions when we have to get up in front of an audience. These inhibitions are simply the manifestation of a response to a strange situation. We become tense, as we do in any fearful situation. Those same hands that moved about so freely and effortlessly when we were conversing with a friend suddenly are bound by some invisible force. Our first impulse is to get them out of sight. So we thrust them into our pockets (where they will probably begin to jingle coins and keys), we lock them behind our backs, we hide them in our armpits, we clasp them together in front of us in the so-called "figleaf" position, or, if a lectern is handy, we grip it until our knuckles whiten. This may well be one reason why it doesn't "feel natural" to gesture at such times; we have placed our hands and ourselves in a position which inhibits free, spontaneous movement.

Just as we have to assume a stance which will not inhibit movement of the entire body from one point to another on the platform, we have to assume a starting position for the hands and arms which does not inhibit their movement. Obviously, the ideal starting position is to allow the arms to hang freely at the sides. Then when we feel the subconscious urge to gesture, our hands and arms can move naturally into action.

The Language of Gestures

From earliest childhood we begin to acquire a gestural "vocabulary." Some of these gestures seem to be instinctive—we offer, we refuse, we beseech—while others we learn from observation of our parents or companions. Soon we have acquired a large stock of gestures which have a conventional meaning for everyone in our environment. Let us review briefly those which are commonly employed by experienced speakers.

The pointing index finger can be used to indicate direction. In addition, the public speaker also employs it for purposes of emphasis. President Kennedy made frequent use of the pointing gesture in his news conferences when he wanted to "underline" a point. The pointed forefinger when held in a vertical position and moved back and forth like an inverted pendulum is commonly associated with caution or warning.

"So it's a question of man controlling machine or machine controlling man." Statements such as the preceding which suggest division or antithesis are commonly accompanied by a gesture in which the hand is held in a vertical position and moved from left to right or right to left. The same gesture can be used in conjunction with a transitional statement such as, "We turn now from the wholesaler to the retailer."

In addition to these familiar conventional gestures, the speaker may employ an endless variety of descriptive gestures which suggest size, shape, texture, and movement.

Thus far we have discussed gestures of the hands and arms. It should be noted that the head and shoulders are instruments for gesticulation as well. We have nodded the head to indicate agreement or shaken it from side to side to indicate disagreement, and perhaps we have used vigorous shakes of the head to indicate emphasis.

FACIAL EXPRESSION

Perhaps the most revealing visual signal that the speaker sends comes from his face. From his facial expression we form impressions of the speaker's attitude toward us, toward himself, and toward his subject. His expression may tell us "I like you people," "I'm really enthusiastic about my topic," "I believe what I'm saying," or it may tell us just the opposite. It may depict a wide range of emotions from fear to confidence, from joy to sadness. Tiny subtleties of expression of which we may not be consciously aware are telling us that one speaker's animation is sincerely motivated, that another speaker's animation is feigned. It is probably no coincidence that the speaker who lacks facial expression generally lacks all animation, visual and vocal. If this lack of animation stems from apathy toward the ideas being expressed, the solution would seem to be to abandon the speech rather than to affect a display of animation. While the affected animation might gain attention, it would result in the audience being conscious of the affectation rather than the ideas of the speech. On the other hand, if the lack of animation results from inhibition rather than from apathy, then the answer lies essentially in placing oneself in the proper psychological attitude. You will find, too, that if you put the rest of your body into action, the face will probably follow suit.

Facial activity, like activity of the hands, arms, and of the body as a whole, is an important factor of attention. Psychologists tell us that as listeners we tend to imitate the physical set of the speaker to whom we are listening. If his facial expression is listless, we tend to assume a listless feeling which may result in inattention to the ideas of the speech. The monotony of expression may exert a sedative effect that literally puts us to sleep unless the speech possesses other more dominant factors of attention.

LIMITATIONS UPON USE OF ACTIONS

Now that we have suggested ways in which bodily action can be utilized to reinforce the verbal elements of the message, we should make note of several limitations upon its use.

1. *Bodily action should be sincerely motivated.* To gesture effectively you must *feel* like gesturing. If you force yourself to employ action when you don't feel like it, the audience can usually detect the artifice. The audience equates this artificiality with insincerity. That is why it is well for the beginning speaker to avoid using planned actions—he is apt to concentrate upon the actions rather than the ideas he is uttering. There is a time, of course, to make conscious use of movements, gestures and facial expressions, and that is during practice sessions.

2. *Bodily action should not be overused.* Most of us have certain favorite actions we like to employ for emphasis, but if we're not careful, we overwork them; so our listeners begin to notice the actions rather than the ideas they are supposed to emphasize. By cultivating a greater variety of actions we will be less likely to overwork any one action.

3. *Bodily action should be appropriate to the occasion.* The same speech can often be delivered in several ways, depending upon the circumstances under which it is delivered. For example, if we are speaking in a large room where there may be some distance between the speaker and the most remote section of the audience, we will have to make our actions more pronounced so that they can be clearly seen. If we have a small, intimate room, our actions will be subtler (and probably fewer in number). Careful analysis of the audience and occasion will reveal the extent to which use should be made of the visible aspects of delivery.

VOCAL ASPECTS OF COMMUNICATION

While part of the speaker's message may be conveyed by visual means, it is by sound—vocalized sound—that the linguistic elements of the message are carried. But, the voice does more than simply render a word-symbol into audible form; it enables the speaker to impart various shades of meaning to that spoken word. Moreover the speaker's voice, like his posture, movements, gestures, and facial expressions, tells things about him quite apart from the verbal message he is uttering. For these reasons, then, we need to sharpen our awareness of the capabilities of the voice to help or hinder our attempts at oral communication.

Voice and Word Meaning

Let us examine first how our vocal behavior affects the *sense* of what we utter. If we were to take the sentence, "Jones is a Democrat," and shift the point of emphasis from one word to another, we could come up with a variety of meanings:

> JONES is a Democrat (but Smith isn't).
> Jones IS a Democrat (my hunch was right).
> Jones is a DEMOCRAT (not a Republican).

Or note how inflectional variations modify the meaning of the simple word, "oh."

> "Oh?" (Really?)
> "Oh." (I get the point.)
> "Oh!" (How exciting!)
> Ohhhh!" (How revolting!)

These examples illustrate the importance of vocal behavior in adding dimension to the meaning of spoken words. The rate that we utter words, the degree of intensity we impart to each one, the variations in pitch we employ, the harshness or mellowness of the sound of each word—all add shades of meaning to the spoken word, just as punctuation marks, special type faces, and indentations modify the meaning of the written word.

Voice and Personality

Not only does the speaker's voice affect the meaning of his message, it also affects the audience's impression of the speaker as a person. In fact, it may very well evoke a misleading impression of the speaker as a person. A thin weak voice may hide a person of vigor and courage. A monotonous voice may hide a man with great inner enthusiasm. The great Greek orator, Demothenes, undoubtedly realized that his speech impediment communicated a false impression of his true worth, so he labored hard to overcome the impediment. It may also be pointed out that a voice ringing with sincerity and enthusiasm may conceal the most unscrupulous sophist.

A word of caution to both speaker and listener is in order at this point. The listener must not be hasty in equating the tone of a man's voice with his character and personality; the voice may be part of a mask hiding the real identity of the speaker and his remarks. The speaker, in turn, must realize that he is judged not only by his words but by meanings that listeners attach to the sound of the voice that carries those words.

Voice and Attention

Earlier in this chapter we observed that movement is a factor of attention, and we noted how movement of the body as a whole, movement of the hands and arms, and movement of the facial muscles all served to keep the audience attentive. This attention factor of movement or activity is applicable to vocal behavior as well. The voice that moves—or more accurately, the voice that is *varied*—holds attention. The speaker who fails to vary his pitch level, or his volume, or his speed, or his tone quality will have difficulty sustaining audience attention for any appreciable length of time unless his message is especially compelling. Of course, vocal variations should always be properly motivated. It would be ludicrous, for example, suddenly to alter your rate of speaking just for the sake of gaining attention. That would only call attention to your use of the device. No delivery technique should call attention to itself; *it should direct attention to the message.*

MECHANICS OF VOICE PRODUCTION

Before we examine those elements of voice which influence word meaning, personality projection, and attention we should have some acquaintance with the way in which vocalized sound is produced. The process is reducible to these four steps: respiration, phonation, resonance, and articulation.

Respiration

Before sound can be produced, a column of air must be forced across the vocal folds in order to set them into vibration. This moving column of air is produced by the organs of respiration in the following manner. During the cycle of inhalation, a series of muscles causes the chest cavity to expand both horizontally and vertically, thus lowering the air pressure inside the lungs. Air then rushes in from the outside to fill the partial vacuum that has been created, thereby equalizing the air pressure in the lungs with that outside the body. During the cycle of exhalation, our muscles cause the chest cavity to contract in both its horizontal and vertical dimensions, thus expelling air from the lungs. It is during this cycle of exhalation that we produce the moving column of air needed for speech. When we are not attempting to produce a vocalized sound, we allow the air to be expelled freely. During speech, we control its expulsion both in terms of amount and in terms of pressure. One of the muscles chiefly instrumental in controlling respiration is the diaphragm, a dome-shaped muscle which separates the thoracic cavity from the visceral cavity. Its downward and upward movements alter the vertical dimensions of the chest cavity, and the rapidity of its movements play an important part in determining the pressure with which we expel air from the lungs.

Phonation

This is the process that takes place when the moving column of air sets the vocal folds into vibration. The VOCAL FOLDS may be thought of as sentries guarding the entrance to the lower respiratory tract. They are located atop the windpipe or trachea in that cartilaginous mid-region of the neck which we call the larynx. During normal breathing they stand apart so that air can move freely in either direction. During speech these vocal folds come together and a column of air under pressure is forced between them, setting them into vibration and producing sound waves.

These vocal folds have several properties which affect the pitch, or frequency, of the vibrations they produce. They can be tensed or relaxed, lengthened or shortened, varied in their thickness in order to produce changes in pitch.

Resonance

The sound waves produced by the vibrating vocal folds would hardly be audible without the resonating cavities and surfaces to amplify them. The principal resonating cavities are in the nose, throat, and mouth, while the bony structure of the head and chest provides resonating surfaces. These resonating cavities and surfaces reinforce the sound waves produced by our vibrating vocal folds in much the same manner as the body of a violin reinforces the sound waves produced by a vibrating string. An important difference between the violin resonators and the vocal resonators is that the latter may, in part, be modified at will. We are speaking of the nasal, oral, and pharyngeal cavities. The latter two cavities, in particular, may be altered in size and shape by muscular action.

Not only do our resonators reinforce the sound waves, they are also instrumental in lending to our voice that distinctive quality which makes it different from that of the next person. Because our resonating cavities may be modified in size and shape, our vocal quality may be modified as well.

Articulation

By means of our resonators we may reinforce sound waves to the point where they can be heard by the listener. But we do not have meaningful speech until we complete the fourth step, articulation. By means of the organs of articulation—the lips, teeth, tongue, palate, and jaw—we modify the "raw" sound into the meaningful oral symbols which we call spoken words.

CONTROLLABLE ELEMENTS OF VOICE

If our vocal behavior fails to gain and hold attention, fails to enhance word meaning, or fails to project a positive impression of personality, we tend to place the blame upon Nature. The popular lament is, "I just wasn't born with a good voice!" Undeniably, Nature does impose limitations upon us. Perhaps the vocal equipment we are born with is inferior to that of our neighbors. But it is in the *use* of the equipment that we are more apt to find the cause of success or failure. Much of our vocal effectiveness depends upon the way in which we control the loudness, pitch, quality, rate, distinctness, and correctness of the sounds we produce.

Loudness

One of the first requisites of vocal sound is that it be loud enough for comfortable hearing. An audience may be willing to exert extra effort in order to hear a person with a weak voice, if that person has something compelling to say. Even so, it is likely that the sheer physical exertion of straining to hear the speaker will ultimately cause the listener to abandon further effort. If, on the other hand, a speaker talks at a painfully loud intensity level, the listener will be more concerned with the discomfort of the sound than the meaning of the sound.

While attaining a comfortable loudness level should be our first concern, we must not overlook the need for *changes* in loudness level. It is by varying our loudness that we enhance word meaning and sustain attention. A speech delivered without variations in loudness is analogous to a symphony played without *crescendo* or *diminuendo*.

Changes in loudness are particularly helpful in providing emphasis to words or phrases. Uttering a word at an intensity level different from that used with the other words in a sentence will direct audience attention to its importance. While such emphasis may be attained by making the sound suddenly louder or softer, recent research suggests that a sudden change to a softer level is apt to be the more effective means of emphasis.

Pitch

The rate of vibration of the vocal folds determines the pitch of the voice. The slower the vibration, the lower the "key." The faster the vibration, the higher the "key." The length and thickness of your vocal folds will determine the extremes of pitch which your voice is capable of producing. Persons with vocal folds of relatively great length and thickness, for example, will probably have bass voices. Whether our natural pitch range may be classified as bass, tenor, or soprano, we have a great flexibility of pitch levels within that range. When we wish to produce a higher note, a series of muscles causes our vocal folds to stretch, much in the same manner as we might stretch a rubber band. A lower note is produced by relaxing these same muscles.

Changes in pitch level within our normal range provide us with one of the most effective means of gaining attention and imparting meaning to utterance. Yet under the duress of a formal speaking situation some people may inhibit their natural tendency to vary the pitch level. The resultant effect, which we call monotony, robs their words of much meaning and exerts a sedative effect upon the listeners' attention. There are other people whose voices are monotonous even in informal conversation. Very likely their monotone is the product of long conditioning. For example, a person raised in a family which was opposed to any display of emotion probably learned by example to inhibit animation in his delivery, both in its visual aspects and its vocal aspects. (Note how often a "poker face" and a monotonous voice go together.)

Quality

Quality is usually expressed in such terms as *strident, rasping, aspirate, mellow, harsh, orotund,* and a variety of other descriptive labels. The speaker's vocal quality can be one of the most obvious signs of his emotional attitude at the moment of speaking. The speaker who is nervous usually tenses his throat muscles inadvertently and the resulting voice quality is apt to be thin and strident. As he relaxes, his throat cavity enlarges, and voice quality becomes much more pleasant. When we grow angry our voice quality becomes harsh and aspirate; when we grow nostalgic and indulge in reverie the voice takes on an almost whispery quality.

If the speaker truly *feels* the meaning of what he is saying, his voice quality will usually take on those characteristics which the audience associates with the sentiment he is expressing.

Rate

Intelligibility, meaning, and attention are all affected by the speaker's rate of utterance. If his rate is too fast, intelligibility may suffer. If his rate is slow when it should be fast or fast when it should be slow, meaning may suffer. Or if his rate is not varied, attention may wane.

We measure rate in terms of the number of words we utter per minute. It is generally agreed that 125 to 150 words per minute constitutes a satisfactory rate for public speaking, but modifications must be made to adapt to room acoustics, audience reactions, the atmosphere of the occasion, and most importantly, to the material of the speech.

Two factors which influence our rate of speaking are *pause* and *duration of sound.* The pause can be one of our most effective oral "punctuation marks." It does for the spoken word what the comma, colon, parenthesis, and dash do for the written word. The misplaced pause, the vocalized pause, or the pause which signals a mental blank can mar a speech that is otherwise effective. *Duration* refers to the time consumed in uttering vowel and consonant sounds. The duration of vowel sounds in particular affects word meaning. To illustrate, utter the word "long," holding the vowel sound but briefly; now, utter the word again, prolonging the vowel sound. The emotional coloration of words is thus modified by changes in duration.

The number of words we utter per minute is, then, dependent upon how much time we spend in pausing (or hesitating) as well as in actually producing the individual sounds of each word. If you are accused of talking too fast or too slow, try to ascertain whether the problem is faulty management of duration or of pause. It is not unusual for a person, when asked to slow down his rate of speaking, to maintain his usual duration while pausing more often or pausing for longer periods. The real culprit in such cases is often faulty management of duration rather than an excessive number of words per minute. Eighty words per minute may seem excessive if each word is given inadequate duration.

Variety of rate is as important as variety of pitch or loudness. The speaker who seems to be following a metronome in his rate of utterance can cloud meaning and diminish attention almost as quickly as a person with a monotone. Emphasis and mood changes can be effectively expressed by variations in rate. For example, when we wish to emphasize one particular statement of a paragraph, we tend to utter it more slowly than the sentences which precede or follow it. A mood of excitement is usually accompanied by an acceleration in rate; a mood of sobriety, with a slowing down in rate.

Distinctness

The clarity of the sounds we produce, though determined in part by our pitch, loudness, and rate, is determined principally by the way we manage the organs of articulation. Some sounds depend upon precise lip movements, others upon critical placement of the tongue, and still others upon full use of the jaw.

Lip laziness results in the blurred enunciation of such consonants as p, b, v, and f. Tongue placement must be precise for clear production of consonants like t, d, k, and g as well as all of the vowel sounds. The importance of jaw action to clear enunciation can be seen if you try reciting the alphabet through clenched teeth.

In striving for greater precision we must avoid going to the extreme of over-preciseness, which the audience interprets as a sign of affectation. Your speech teacher may offer suggestions for the improvement of your enunciation. If so, get in the habit of implementing these improvements in your everyday conversation; then the demands of the public speaking situation will be much easier to fulfill.

Correctness

While enunciation has to do with the distinctness of a spoken word, pronunciation has to do with its correctness. It is possible to enunciate a word with greatest clarity while grossly mispronouncing it. Faults of pronunciation are less easily forgiven by the audience than faults of enunciation, because they seem to reflect upon the speaker's intelligence rather than upon his muscular dexterity. Let us examine briefly some of the more common errors of pronunciation.

"I dint have any idear that the Eyetalian athalete had a damaged larnix." This highly improbable combination of errors represents five classes of mispronunciation. "Dint" for "didn't" is an example of *sound omission.* Some omissions are to be noted in the middle of words, such as "literchur" for "literature" or "probly" for "probably"; others are noted at the ends of words, particularly those ending with t or d; still others are evident in difficult sound combinations, such as "monce" for "months." *Sound substitution* is evident in the next error in our sample sentence, "idear." Other common substitutions are represented in "aig" for "egg," "jist" for "just," "git" for "get," "ladder" for "latter." *Misplaced accent* is seen in "EYEtalian" and in such other words as "abDOMEn," "GITar," and "REward." "Athalete" represents the *addition of a sound,* as does "yeyus" for "yes" and "Warshington" for "Washington." Probably the least common of the errors, *sound inversion,* is epitomized by "larnix" for "larynx." "Calvary" for "cavalry," and "noo-q-lur" for "noo-KLEE-ur" are other examples.

Probably the most practical method of determining acceptable pronunciation is to listen to the educated speakers in your particular geographic area. What might be considered as acceptable in Atlanta might not be so in Duluth, owing to differences in dialect. With the growing mobility of our society and the spread of mass media of communication, regional differences in pronunciation are becoming less evident.

For the pronunciation of little-used words, names of places, and foreign expressions a good pronouncing dictionary is your most reliable guide. But try to use only the very latest edition, because usage may well change within a few years' time.

TAKING STOCK OF NEEDS

With these general guidelines for using bodily action and vocal variety now before you, take a careful inventory of your current delivery practices in various communication situations. Enlist the aid of friends who will offer candid views of your assets and liabilities in informal conversation, discussions, conferences. Ask your speech instructor for his analysis of your needs in public speaking situations. Try to find answers to questions such as these: To what *degree* do I employ bodily action and effective vocal variety in each of the various communication situations? To an insufficient degree in public speaking, a sufficient degree in conversation? To a distracting degree in some cases? What is the *quality* of the action which I do employ? Does it help or hinder the communication of my ideas? Is it meaningful action? Does it call attention itself? If so, why? Does my posture communicate a positive impression? Does it combine ease with alertness? Are my movements and gestures graceful and decisive, or are they hesitant, tentative, lacking in vigor and enthusiasm? Do I have any annoying mannerisms that should be curbed? Does my use of my voice add to or detract from the communication situation? Securing answers to these and other pertinent questions will enable you to chart your course toward greater effectiveness in the use of visible and audible aspects of communication.

A PHILOSOPHY FOR IMPROVEMENT

As you approach the task of improving your use of voice and bodily action in speaking, bear in mind these words from Dr. Hugh Blair, one of the great speech critics of the eighteenth century:

> If one has naturally any gross defect in his voice or gestures, he begins at the wrong end, if he attempts at reforming them only when he is to speak in public. He should begin with rectifying them in his private manner of speaking; and then carry to the public the right habit he has formed. For when a speaker is engaged in a public discourse, he should not be then employ-

ing his attention about his manner, or thinking of his tones and gestures. If he be so employed, study and affectation will appear. He ought to be then quite in earnest; wholly occupied with his subject and his sentiments; leaving nature, and previously formed habits, to prompt and suggest his manner of delivery.

SUMMARY

For effective oral communication it is essential that the verbal and non-verbal elements of the message work in harmony. The non-verbal elements of the message are visual and vocal. The visual constituents include the speaker's appearance (his dress, his posture, his facial expression) and his bodily actions. Actions convey meaning and help to sustain attention. The speaker should adopt a posture or stance that does not inhibit spontaneous movement. Movement on the platform is generally motivated by a desire to make an idea emphatic or to suggest a transition from one idea to another. The speaker's gestures may be classified as conventional (having a widely-accepted meaning quite apart from the verbal elements of the message), and descriptive (having meaning only when accompanied by the verbal elements). Facial expression is perhaps the most revealing element of the visual aspects of communication. Lack of facial expression may derive from inhibition or apathy but is usually interpreted by the listener as apathy. The speaker's action should be sincerely motivated, should be appropriate to the subject, to the speaker himself, to the audience, and to the occasion, and should not be overused.

The voice does more than simply render a word symbol into audible form. It enables the speaker to impart various shades of meaning to the spoken word, it transmits an impression of the speaker as a person, and it acts as a factor of attention. Voice production can be divided into four stages: respiration, phonation, resonation, and articulation. The controllable elements of the voice are pitch, loudness, rate, and quality. These elements should be varied in a manner consistent with the "sense" of the verbal element of the message. Faults in distinctness of vocal sounds are more readily forgiven than faults in the correctness of the sounds. Among the more common errors of correctness are sound omission, sound substitution, misplaced accent, addition of a sound, and sound inversion. Acceptability of pronunciation varies from region to region. You are advised to emulate the pronunciation of the best educated speakers in your geographical area.

SUGGESTED READINGS

VIRGIL A. ANDERSON, *Training the Speaking Voice*, (New York: Oxford University Press, 1961). Parts I and II.

ARTHUR J. BRONSTEIN, *The Pronunciation of American English*, (New York: Appleton-Century-Crofts, 1960). Chapter 1.

DONALD C. BRYANT and KARL R. WALLACE, *Fundamentals of Public Speaking*, (New York: Appleton-Century-Crofts, Inc., 1953). Chapters 11-15.

GLEN R. CAPP, *How to Communicate Orally*, (Englewood Cliffs, N. J.: Prentice-Hall, 1961). Chapters 10-13.

THEODORE CLEVENGER, JR., "A Synthesis of Experimental Research in Stage Fright," *Quarterly Journal of Speech*, (April, 1959). 134-145.

JOEL R. DAVITZ, ed., *The Communication of Emotional Meaning*, (New York: McGraw-Hill, 1964). Chapters 2-8.

GILES WILKERSON GRAY, and WALDO N. BRADEN, *Public Speaking: Principle and Practice*, (New York: Harper and Brothers, 1951). Chapters 19-22.

E. HAHN, C. LOMAS, D. HARGIS, and D. VANDRAEGEN, *Basic Voice Training for Speech*, (New York: McGraw-Hill, Co., 1952).

ALAN H. MONROE, *Principles and Types of Speech*, (Chicago: Scott, Foresman, 1962). Chapters 4-6.

CHARLES S. MUDD, and MALCOM O. SILLARS, *Speech: Content and Communication*, (San Francisco, Calif.: Chandler Publishing Co., 1960). Chapters 13-15.

ALBERT UPTON, *Design for Thinking*, (Stanford, Calif.: Stanford Press, 1961). Chapter 9.

EVIDENCE

THE FOUNDATION OF YOUR IDEAS

As members of a society which employs communication as a means of sharing experiences, thoughts and feelings, we are constantly telling others about our ideas and beliefs. When we have an idea we wish to share with another party, we endeavor to express that idea clearly and effectively so that the listener will "see what we are talking about." If we desire to change someone's mind we also strive to clarify, amplify and defend our position. It is, indeed, an exhilarating sensation to know that what we asserted is interesting, understandable and believable because we explained, illustrated and demonstrated its merits and usefulness.

What is true with respect to explaining and supporting your ideas in everyday conversation is just as true in public speaking, but more demanding. Just as the builder has certain materials which he uses to construct a house, so you, as a speaker, have to supply the materials for developing main ideas, primary and secondary headings. We all know that simply stating a point does not necessarily render it believable or true. There may be some assertions that listeners will accept at face value because the assertions are consistent with their existing beliefs and prejudices. But more frequently listeners require that assertions be backed up with proof. Recently a speaker on a college campus was advocating that the football team be disbanded on the grounds that it was a financial burden to the student body. Because this charge was merely asserted, and not supported with proof, the speaker's pleas were never heeded. The efficient communicator seeks to support his observations and his positions, and does not depend on chance or fate to win his point. He furnishes the listener with the materials that indicate the assertion to be credible, reliable and clear.

VERBAL SUPPORT

Of all the things one could say on a subject, some will be incidental and irrelevant, others will be fundamental, depending upon how we plan to change the listener's behavior. One of the basic tasks of the speaker is to look hard at his subject until he can recognize those elements in it that are clearly pertinent and essential to accomplishing his purpose. Those elements which serve to establish the position being advanced by the speaker we may call the FORMS OF SUPPORT.

Consider some of the forms of support that are available to the speaker when he thinks it is necessary and beneficial to clarify or prove an assertion.

Illustration (Example)

From the earliest days of man's history, the story-teller has commanded and held attention. His use of the narrative as a device for proving, clarifying and maintaining interest has been discussed by writers of communication from Aristotle to the present. The very fact that a story or an example holds our attention renders it an excellent tool in many communication situations.

An illustration is the narration of a happening or incident which amplifies, proves or clarifies the point under consideration. It is, in a sense, the speaker saying to the audience, "Here is an example of what I mean." In addition, it often aids memory in that it makes the important features more noteworthy.

The illustration usually takes one of three forms—THE DE-TAILED FACTUAL ILLUSTRATION, THE UNDEVELOPED FACTUAL ILLUS-TRATION (SPECIFIC INSTANCE), AND THE HYPOTHETICAL ILLUSTRA-TION. Some overlapping may occur as the speaker limits or expands his details.

THE DETAILED, FACTUAL ILLUSTRATION USUALLY TAKES THE FORM OF A NARRATIVE (STORY) WHICH ANSWERS THE QUESTIONS WHO? WHAT? WHERE? WHEN? AND HOW? Because of the detail in the story, and because the story is true, the illustration is both vivid and meaningful to the audience. The knowledge that something actually occurred is a source of interest. Notice how our interest is stirred when we hear someone say, "Let me tell you of a case that actually happened."

A student in a speech class recently made good use of the detailed, factual illustration in a talk dealing with seat belts. The speaker was trying to convince the audience that seat belts can save lives.

> A friend of mine, Tom Overstreet, was returning to San Diego after spending a weekend in Los Angeles. He was driving on U.S. 101 when his car blew a tire and started weaving from lane to lane. Finally he lost control of his car as it headed for the soft shoulder. Instead of stopping at the shoulder the car rolled off the road and started to turn over and over. The car rolled over three times before it came to rest. Tom was wearing his seat belt during the ordeal and therefore managed to remain inside his car.
>
> The police officer that arrived at the scene told Tom that his seat belt kept him from being killed, or at least from sustaining serious injury.

Still another speaker used a factual illustration in an attempt to establish the premise that teaching by television is often more effective than the traditional methods. He told, in detail, of the success of a college class in anthropology that was taught by television, and how the students in this class learned more than those students enrolled in the classes taught in the usual manner.

Through such illustrations the speaker is able to have the audience see and experience the point he is trying to make. Because it is limited to but one example, the illustration often serves as the springboard for the presentation of additional and more specific examples.

In utilizing the detailed, factual illustration it is worthwhile to keep a few criteria in mind. First, see to it that your example relates directly to your point. It is often a   temptation to use an illustration simply because it is a "good story." If the audience has a difficult time seeing the connection between your assertion and your illustration, confusion may result. Second, use sufficient detail, clothed in image-evoking language, so that your illustration holds the interest of the audience. Third, be accurate. Avoid making your narrative a mixture of truth and fiction. Fourth, use the factors of attention discussed in Chapter VII as a means of making your illustrations appealing to the audience.

The undeveloped factual illustration is an example that omits much of the detail and development which characterizes the extended factual illustration. Several such brief, condensed examples may be advanced by the speaker as a means of indicating the widespread nature of the situation or suggesting the frequency of an occurrence. The main advantage of the undetailed example is that since it is short and takes little time to present, it allows the speaker an opportunity to present a great deal of proof material in a minimum amount of time. For instance, if one is asserting that there is a shortage of high school teachers in California, he might establish his point by stating: "In San Diego there was a shortage of eighty-two high school teachers in 1967. Los Angeles found that they were unable to fill one-hundred and forty-six positions in their high schools. San Francisco was also short ninety-seven teachers the same year." In talking about the value of a college honor system, your cause would be aided by saying, "The University of Indiana has found the honor system successful. Purdue University and the University of California at Davis have also reported satisfactory results from the honor system." By using actual people, places, events, and things you are making the material both meaningful and persuasive.

Some examples may require only one word, like the name of a town or a person, while others may call for a sentence or two. In any case the use of undeveloped illustrations adds strength and understanding to an idea. They provide excellent proof, and are often most effective when they directly follow a detailed factual illustration. For example, a student who wanted to prove that a recent automobile strike had adversely affected the workers supported his position by relating the true story of an actual worker and his family. The speaker then bolstered his case by citing a number of undeveloped factual illustrations involving other workers.

The hypothetical illustration is a detailed fictional illustration which seeks to let the audience see "what could be" or what they might "suppose." It is most often used as a method of depicting future events or of making the future seem graphically clear.

If a speaker were discussing the dangers of invading Cuba, he might use a hypothetical illustration by asking his audience to imagine a raging battle on a Cuban beach. In a speech dealing with a proposal to raise school taxes the speaker might offer a hypothetical illustration of how the proposal would affect the audience. Or, a speaker might offer a detailed illustration to convince his listeners that high school drop-outs have a difficult time securing employment:

> Suppose a friend of yours in high school decides that he has had enough school. He is doing poorly in Math and English and therefore feels there is no real need to finish the semester. On Saturday he asks the owner of a local market to give him a job. The market owner can pay only fifty dollars a week. But your friend, having never made that much money decides to take the job instead of reporting back to school on Monday.
>
> After about two weeks on the job he is dismissed. Business is off at the store and the owner can't afford any extra help. Your friend then goes from store to store, and from factory to factory, looking for some sort of employment. But he soon dis-

covers that employers are not interested in hiring someone without at least a high school education. Your friend, in essence, is unable to find work because he left school.

Depicting the future with the illustration can place the listener in a situation that affects him personally and emotionally. A statement such as "What happens if you reject this plan?" affords the speaker an opportunity to place the listener in the center of a hypothetical picture.

In using the hypothetical illustration the speaker should keep a few key points in mind. First, the speaker can select any story he wants when he uses a hypothetical illustration, but he should never present an imaginary story as being true-to-fact. Employing phrases such as "imagine a situation such as this," or "suppose you discover . . ." will allow the listener to separate fact from fiction. Second, if the hypothetical illustration is going to be effective, it should be reasonable and capable of happening. An illustration that is an obvious exaggeration might well offend the watchful listener. Third, always remember that an imaginary story proves very little. Therefore, the student of communication should try to locate a factual example if he is trying to prove a point, and rely on the hypothetical illustration if he is trying to clarify a point or arouse the emotions. Fourth, in using the hypothetical example, like the factual, make certain that it is appropriate and related directly to the point in question. The story must not be in the speech for its own sake, but rather for the purpose of supporting and/or clarifying some idea.

Testing Examples and Illustrations

If one is going to be confronted with examples, both as a speaker and as a listener, he must be sure that the examples meet certain requirements. When one employs an example or an illustration he may be asking the listener to draw a conclusion from the specific illustration. For instance, someone might try to condemn all California drivers because of a situation he experienced while driving on a Los Angeles freeway. In drawing the generalization from the specific example the speaker is suggesting that the example supports his position. Therefore, the following precautions should be observed whenever you use or listen to examples and illustrations that are presented as a justification for a specific hypothesis.

1. *Are there enough examples to justify the generalization?* There can be, of course, no absolute measure of "enough" in applying this test. The answer depends on many factors, but largely upon the phenomena being discussed. If the conclusion being drawn is somewhat controversial and primarily a value judgement, one should expect more than one or two illustrations. Someone telling you of a friend who was beaten and robbed in New York would not be in a position to establish the premise that New York streets are dangerous with that single example.

2. *Is the example or illustration a typical case?* Too often people try to change our beliefs and opinions by offering us as proof an example that is, under closer examination, an isolated case. It would be unfair, for example, to judge the entire membership of a fraternity by the experience of one person.

3. *Is the example clearly relevant to the idea?* When we talked about critical listening in Chapter III we suggested that the careful listener learns to ask "So what?" to certain information. Checking the relevancy of examples is merely an extension of that idea. If you were talking about the dangers of night driving and cited only an illustration of someone whose brakes failed, you would be guilty of offering an irrelevant case.

4. *Is the illustration properly detailed and explained?* There are times when the illustration used lacks sufficient detail, and therefore may not contain the essential material. If you were talking of smoking and lung cancer, you might hurt your cause if you were to tell of a man who died of cancer, while at the same time forgetting to tell us anything about his smoking habits.

5. *Is there other evidence to support the conclusion being made by the generalization?* This test should be applied to any evidence, whether it is presented in the form of an illus-

tration, statistics, testimony or analogy. Before we are satisfied that the example proves the specific point we should ask for other facts and authoritative opinions which might suggest the falsity or validity of the generalization. Suppose, for example, that you are urging reforms in college registration procedures and have offered a single illustration to substantiate the need for reforms. Your position will be enhanced if you will offer additional support—such as citing remarks of the Dean of Admissions which add believability to your thesis.

Statistics

In a sense, statistics are examples. Instead of talking about one or two cases or instances, we attempt to measure and define things quantitatively. Statistics are facts represented numerically; they compare or show proportions as a means of helping a speaker develop and prove a point. Used in this way statistics help compress, summarize, and simplify the facts that relate to the issue in question. The essential characteristic of statistics is that they are simply generalizations derived from comparisons of individual instances.

Statistics, like illustrations, may be brief or quite detailed. The mere citation of a figure, such as the statement, "Medical authorities estimate that there are approximately 30,000 hemophiliacs of all types in the United States," would be considered statistics. There are also occasions when the statistics take a much longer form. When discussing the 1965 Mayor's race in New York City a speaker used the following statistics:

> And who is winning? At the week's end the *New York Herald Tribune* using a previously untested street-corner polling system, showed Democrat Abraham Beam far ahead of Republican John Lindsay, 44.2% to 36%, with Conservative Bill Buckley at 12.6%. The New York Daily News poll, which has a relatively good record of accurate political prediction over 37 years, gave Lindsay 42.4%, Beam 41.1% and Buckley, 16.5%.

Both of these examples indicate that speakers can use statistics to make ideas clear, interesting, and impelling.

Since statistics are a strong method of proof, they should
be gathered and presented in the most effective manner possible. The following few rules may increase your efficiency.

1. Whenever possible present your statistics as round numbers, especially when several are offered. It is much easier to
remember the population of a city if we hear "one and a half
million," instead of "1,512,653." There are, of course, certain
instances where exactness is essential. The purpose for which
the statistics are being used should be the main factor in making your selection.

2. Give specific and complete source citations for your
statistics. Saying "these statistics prove that . . ." or "quoting
from a reliable source . . ." does not tell your audience where
you located your information. If the material is controversial, it
is useful to cite the magazine or book, specific pages and the
date. In most cases, however, the date and the name of the
magazine will be sufficient—for example, "According to the
June 14, 1967 issue of *Time* magazine . . ." The act of docu-
mentation adds to the credibility and acceptability of your
arguments.

3. Avoid presenting too many statistics. A speech crammed
with numbers often results in confusion and lack of attention.

4. Make certain that your statistics directly relate to the
point you are making and see that this relationship is clearly
recognized by the listeners.

Testing Statistics

Statistics can have a telling effect on an audience as they
listen to the comprehensiveness inherent in most statistical
data. When used with factual examples this comprehensiveness is combined with concreteness. Unfortunately, however,
statistics are highly liable to error and abuse. The conscientious speaker, as well as the critical and careful listener, must
therefore be willing to apply certain criteria to the statistics
he confronts. _Testing STATS_

1. *Are the units being compared actually comparable?* It
may be said that city X has twenty-five more crimes than does
city Y, but if city X counts all crime and city Y counts only

crimes against people and not those against property, the statistics are unreliable. In addition, city X may have a population of one-hundred thousand, while city Y has only thirty-five thousand residents. In both of these cases the units compared are not compatible.

2. *Do the statistics cover a sufficient number of cases?* A statement that fifty percent of the voters polled favored Proposition II would be quite misleading if only ten people out of forty-thousand were asked their opinion.

3. *Do the statistics cover a sufficient period of time?* There are really two considerations in applying this test. First, if one is going to talk about the high cost of foreign aid he must give current statistics. The foreign aid bill changes each year, and what was valid five years ago is likely to be outdated today. In short, use current references whenever possible. Second, if you wish to draw conclusions from your data, you must be sure that the period covered is not exceptional. The flow of mail in December, unemployment figures in summer and winter, earnings of some companies during war time, and traffic after a football game are obviously exceptional cases.

4. *Are the statistics presented in a logical form?* Often a speaker will jump from percentages to raw scores without any explanation. When talking about the political make-up of New York City a speaker noted:

> City census figures show 15% of New Yorkers are Negro, 8% Puerto Rican, 11% Italian, 4% Irish. There are an estimated 1,800,000 Jews, 3,400,000 Roman Catholics, and 1,700,-000 Protestants. And there are 3½ times as many registered Democrats as Republicans.

Notice that the speaker offers three different sets of numbers in one passage, and each set is presented in a manner different from the other sets.

5. *Were the gatherers of the statistics strongly interested in the outcome?* Whenever you gather and analyze evidence it is crucial that you examine the bias and attitudes found within the special groups that originally compiled the data. For example, if you were considering the cost of living and

union membership in states with the "Right to Work Law," you might find different results as you approached the Bureau of Labor Statistics, the AFL-CIO, the Democratic National Committee and the National Association of Manufacturers. In these instances the speaker should consider as many different sources as possible and try to locate a neutral source.

Testimony

In the complex world we live in it has become impossible for someone to be an authority on all topics. We have become increasingly dependent upon the expert testimony of others as a way of helping us find the relevant facts on an issue or a concept. The public speaker must also, on many occasions, turn to an expert. The testimony of an authority, as a form of support for a specific point, is often the most important type of evidence a speaker can use. It can show that the opinions of persons of authority, or experts in the field, corroborate the speaker's own views. For example, if you were trying to convince an audience that periodic chest X-rays could save lives, you might quote the testimony of the Surgeon General of the United States: "Our office has long held to the belief that systematic and regular chest X-rays could help save the lives of many cancer and TB victims." A speaker giving a talk for the purpose of convincing an audience that the ex-convict has a difficult time re-entering society used expert testimony in the following manner:

> Lester N. Smith, who served as Head Warden of Sing Sing prison for eleven years, indicated the scope of the problem faced by the ex-convict when he stated that society rejects the convict right down the line. It is hard for him to locate a job, almost impossible to own a home, and difficult to lead a normal life. The labor unions often bar him and big companies fear him. In a very real sense, he finds most roads back to a normal life filled with social and economic blocs.

Your use of testimony can be made more effective by observing some simple rules.

1. In selecting experts it is helpful to select those individuals that will carry considerable weight with your audience. You

should in all circumstances establish the speaker's credibility and explain to your audience why he is an expert. That is, make it clear to your listeners that this particular person should be respected.

2. Cite complete sources when using testimony. Let the listeners know where you found your evidence, whether it be magazine, book, newspaper, television program or personal interview.

3. Don't try to memorize your quotations. By reading your quotations directly you can assure accuracy and also avoid forgetting. In addition, reading small portions of your speech, such as some of your evidence, will offer your audience a change of pace. Furthermore, the act of reading a particular quotation will enhance its credibility. A small card will not detract from your speech if you handle it correctly.

4. The testimony should be relevant to the point being discussed. Speakers will often cite an authority to prove a position, but on closer examination it is discovered that the expert is talking about another problem. At times it is necessary for the speaker to explain the relevancy in his own language.

5. Avoid lifting the quotation out of context in such a way that the meaning intended by the expert is seriously altered.

6. Whenever possible use quotations that are brief. Quotations that are long are often quite difficult to follow and on occasion hinder the audience's ability to concentrate. Even when paraphrasing you should aim at brevity.

7. Attend carefully to the means of introducing quotations. Lead-ins such as "In a speech last week Secretary of State Dean Rusk noted . . ." and "So we see, as Professor Jones pointed out, over-population and food shortage present serious problems . . ." will help hold the audience's attention at the same time that they tell the source of the quotation and the time that it was delivered.

8. Indicate the beginning and the end of any quotation so that the audience will be able to distinguish your opinions from those of the expert you are quoting. However, try to

avoid the all-too-common practice of "quote" and "unquote." A change of voice, a pause, a move, or a certain phrase can indicate the beginning and end of a quotation.

Testing Testimony

In using and listening to testimony you should always remember that an expert's opinion may not be based on any concrete and comprehensive evidence. There are some safeguards one should observe whenever expert testimony is being used.

1. *Is the authority being quoted recognized as an expert in his field?* A common error today is to judge people as experts in many areas because they happen to be particularly qualified in one field. A college professor may teach 18th Century English Literature, but this does not qualify him as an expert in economic affairs. The person's training, background, and degrees are one indication, but common sense and critical judgement are additional tests of expert testimony and qualification.

2. *Is the person an unbiased observer?* Objectivity is essential if we are to respect and believe the testimony of the expert. The chairman of the Republican National Committee would hardly be qualified to give an objective and accurate account of a Democratic President's term in office.

3. *Is the reference to authority specific?* Quotations such as "according to an eminent authority," or "an expert in the field concluded," are vague and misleading. We should know exactly *who* is being quoted.

4. *Are the opinions and feelings being expressed supported by other authorities and other evidence?* If one looks hard enough and long enough, he can find testimony on all sides of a question and on all subjects, but careful and thorough investigation will reveal whether or not the expert is all alone in his views.

5. *When and where was the opinion expressed?* We live in such a changing and dynamic society that statistics, theories, and findings are soon out-dated. What an expert said in 1963 may not express his views today. In addition, the place a

statement is made may well influence what is said. The Secretary of Labor might well state one view at the Teamsters convention and yet expound still another position, on the same theme, before the Chamber of Commerce.

Analogy or Comparison

We are constantly asking someone to compare one idea or item with another. In trying to make our ideas clear, interesting and impelling we suggest that item A "resembles," "is similar to," or "is not as good as" item B. By using comparison we try to support our main thesis and explain our principal ideas.

Comparison usually takes the form of an ANALOGY. In using an analogy, similarities are pointed out in regard to people, ideas, experiences, projects, institutions, or data, and conclusions are drawn on the basis of those similarities. The main function of the analogy is to point out the similarities between that which is already known and that which is not. In using this technique as support or proof, you should show the listener that what he already believes or knows is similar to what you are trying to prove or explain. For example, if you are suggesting that it is dangerous to drive while intoxicated you might offer the following analogy:

> We all know that if someone drives while wearing a blindfold his vision is greatly obscured and his life is in danger (known). The same can be said of the person who tries to drive a car after he has been drinking. His vision is also obscured and his life is indeed in real danger (unknown).

Ordinarily, analogies are divided into two types: FIGURATIVE and LITERAL. The FIGURATIVE compares things of different classes; such as the United States Banking System with a man's circulatory system, or an airplane with a bird. To say that writing a term paper is like driving a car, because both have certain basic rules that are difficult at first and get easier with time, would be an example of a figurative analogy. This type of analogy is generally vivid, full of imagery, but has limited value as proof, since the dissimilarities of things in different classes are usually obvious and can be readily attacked—often to the disadvantage of the creator of the analogy.

Much more useful and valid is the LITERAL analogy, whereby you compare items, ideas, institutions, people, projects, data, or experiences of the same class. You might point out similarities between one instructor and another, one political creed and another, or one city and another. On the basis of the similarities you build up a theorem. We reason that if two or more things of the same class contain identical or nearly identical characteristics, certain conclusions that are true in one case may also be true in the other(s). For example, Winston Churchill employed a literal analogy when he compared the turning point of the Civil War with what he believed to be the turning point in World War II. Still another example can be found in the speaker who was trying to persuade an audience that the United Nations Charter should be obeyed by all member nations:

> We Americans take a great deal of pride in the Constitution and the Bill of Rights. We know that our country would not be as great and as strong as it is if we were to discontinue our obedience and allegiance to the laws and regulations contained in these documents. The same can be said of the United Nations Charter. For just as each of us, as individuals, must comply with the Constitution and its provisions, so must the members of the United Nations comply with its laws and rules. If the individual nations do not observe and obey the laws of the Charter of the United Nations, it will not be an effective instrument for world peace.

The comparison and similarities are obvious—we are aware of the concepts behind the Constitution (known), the speaker suggests that the same concepts are inherent to the United Nations Charter (unknown). In summary, you believe and understand one, therefore, you should believe and understand the other, for they are basically the same.

Testing Analogy

In selecting and using analogies, either figurative or literal, it is essential that your analogies meet certain requirements.

1. _Is the analogy clearly relevant to the idea?_ To argue that since John and Tom both belong to the same social organization they must therefore think the same way politically, is an example of irrelevant use of analogy. The similarity of their organization may be interesting, but is certainly not relevant.

2. _Do the points of likeness outweigh the points of difference?_ If the differences, on the _essential_ features being compared, outweigh the similarities, one can hardly establish a logical connection. If one compares a supermarket to a high school, in order to make the point that each must keep its customers, he has overlooked some fundamental differences that exist in the two cases.

3. _Is the premise (generalization) upon which the analogy is based accurate?_ Saying "just as a ship sinks without a captain, so will our club be destroyed without a president," is an example of a false circumstance being used as a basis for the generalization. For a ship does not necessarily sink without a captain. The premise for the entire analogy and conclusion is therefore inaccurate and invalid.

4. _Is the analogy appropriate to the audience?_ It is important for the audience to observe clearly the likenesses and the essential characteristics of the analogy. If one-half of the comparison confuses your listeners, you may find that your analogy has hindered instead of aided your speech.

5. _Is the analogy supported by other forms of support?_ Analogies alone are seldom sufficient to prove a point. You should try to examine other types of evidence to see if the relationship between the known and the unknown can be verified.

Other Forms of Support

At the beginning of this chapter we made note of the fact that the forms of support occasionally overlapped—that a factual illustration might well contain statistics. Certain other forms of support are closely related to the six already discussed. Many of these are further extensions and refinements of those just mentioned. For example, the ANECDOTE, in which real-life characters are usually featured, the FABLE, in which animal characters speak and act as if they were human beings, and the PARABLE, which is a fictitious story from which a moral or religious lesson may be drawn, are all forms of the illustration. Long quotations, at times, may be listed as a type of testimony.

Other devices for developing, amplifying, and clarifying, such as explanation, definition, restatement, repetition, and description, will be discussed in detail in Chapter X when we examine the principles of informing. There are also many situations where a speaker will use a combination of these devices. For example, you may have occasion to cite an expert who is, in turn, citing statistics or using an analogy. The important concept for the student of communication to remember is that any of the techniques discussed in this book should be used if they will aid in the securing of the response you desire. The various classifications suggested throughout the volume are only a guide for specific occasions; the real communication situation must determine your final selection.

VISUAL SUPPORT

The importance and use of visual aids will be discussed in a very specific manner when we examine the speech to inform in Chapter X. However, visual aids are also useful as a means of supporting and proving an idea, principle or concept. By *seeing* what is being talked about the listener brings still another one of his senses into play. In trying to convince the judge that the stop sign was blocked from view by a large tree, the lawyer brought forth a photograph. On seeing the picture the judge ruled the defendant could not have seen the sign from his car. The old adage "seeing is believing" is made real by a specific chart, model, demonstration, or exhibit. In addition, statistics that are often detailed and confusing can be clarified and reinforced by a graph or table that highlights the main features.

The best advice for both the novice and the professional speaker using visual aids is to *practice*! By practicing with your visual aid you will discover the strengths and weaknesses of the aid before the actual speaking situation occurs. In addition, the conscientious student should try to answer the following questions: (1) Can the audience see the important details contained within the visual aid? Are they large enough and clear enough? (2) Will the visual aid distract the audience? When and how shall I display it? (3) Does my visual aid directly support the point under consideration?

FINDING MATERIAL

Much of the information you use as supporting and clarifying material will come from your personal experience. Illustrations and examples are often drawn from the realm of personal observations. Analogies and hypothetical illustrations can be discovered by using your own creative and imaginative ability. In most situations, however, there will be a need to look elsewhere, to go beyond personal experiences and creative reflections.

Once you have selected your topic and decided on your purpose, the serious task of deciding what you want to say begins. In making decisions concerning your material you must begin by carefully thinking about the audience and your objectives. By placing the topic in its proper perspective you will be better able to determine what you know about the central issues and what you must find out.

Experience and Observation

One of the best ways to gather material for speeches or for everyday conversation is to be alert to what goes on around us. If one goes through life wearing blinders and not taking full advantage of all his senses he is apt to miss much of the detail and information that life can offer. Plato once wrote, "Knowledge is but to remember." To have the experiences and observations to remember one must develop the philosophy of "awareness." Being aware of the world around you is as simple as listening to speeches, listening to news programs, taking part in conversations, and keeping both eyes wide open as you move from environment to environment.

If being aware and alert is part of your daily philosophy, you can call forth personal experiences and first-hand observations for your speeches. These personal examples are often more vivid and lively than those examples you have read about. Therefore, as we suggested earlier, start your speech preparation by discovering your own ideas, beliefs and feelings on the subject. *Examine your memory*.

You should be cautioned, however, about depending solely on the conclusions reached from observations. We all know that our perception of any happening is colored by our background and earlier experiences. This lack of objective perceptiveness can often influence what we *really* see and hear. Therefore, make effective and abundant use of observations and past experiences, but always remember you are dealing with a statistic of one. More proof may be needed for a valid generalization.

Interviews

The experiences and observations of other people, who might be in a better position to know more about the subject than you are often excellent sources of information. The interview has several advantages. First, it enables you to ask specific questions that are directly related to your topic. This face-to-face situation lets you acquire quick responses to your questions. Second, the interview allows you a certain degree of selectivity. Instead of simply talking to someone who knows a little about the topic, you can gather data by going directly to an expert— someone with first hand information.

As a college student you are in a position to make extensive use of interviews. Most professors are experts in specific fields and can offer you some valuable assistance. To illustrate, if you were going to give a speech dealing with the problems of inter-racial marriages, you might gain some useful information and some new ideas from interviews with professors in sociology, psychology, religion, and marriage and family relations. In addition, you might also seek an appointment with some of the campus ministers. In all of these instances you are increasing your background on the topic.

An interview of any kind requires forethought—arranging for the meeting, preparing an agenda, and thinking out the means of securing frank responses. The interviewer should also be on time, explain his purpose, take careful notes and be careful not to misquote the person when the material is used.

Printed Material

Donald C. Bryant and Karl R. Wallace, in their text on oral communication, noted, "The library is to the speechmaker what the laboratory is to the scientist. It is a place of search and research." We would also suggest that reading in books, magazines, periodicals, newspapers, documents and the like constitute the largest single source of information at the disposal of any speaker.

Before recommending some places to look for printed material let us offer some advice for all researchers.

1. Read with a definite purpose. We wrote earlier in this section that your preparation begins after you have decided on your specific purpose and reviewed your personal fund of information. With those two tasks behind you it is much easier to seek out only that material which is relevant. You will also be able to be more selective and avoid going off in many different directions.

2. Read more than you think you will use. Most beginning students feel compelled to read only enough to "get by." You will discover, however, that the most effective speakers have a grasp of the topic which goes beyond the material given in the speech.

3. Be critical. Examine many sources and opinions on the same topic. In this way you will be able to determine the validity of your ideas as well as the authenticity of what you read.

4. Take complete and accurate notes on what you read. It is important, for ethical as well as practical reasons, for you to keep a record of exactly where your material came from. For example, if your material is from a magazine, you should

have the author, title of the article, name of the magazine, volume, date and page. This material is often cited in your speech and shown in your outline and bibliography. You should also use quotation marks when quoting directly. Plagiarism is to be avoided at all times.

5. Know your library. Although similarities exist, no two libraries are alike. Discover what catalog system your library uses, what reference books they have, their physical facilities, their special collections, their regulations and their hours. Feel free to ask questions of those who work in the library. Timidity may well cost you access to some valuable information.

Indexes

The library card catalogue, with its subject, title and author index, is a superb starting point for your research. In this file you will find a complete listing of the books found in your library. *The Reader's Guide to Periodical Literature*, which is published each month, is a cumulative index to articles published in more than a hundred selected periodicals. Articles are listed alphabetically as to author, title, and subject. Two newspapers, *The New York Times* and *The London Times*, are also indexed.

In addition to the common indexes cited above the diligent student might have occasion to consult *The Bulletin of Public Affairs Information Service* and the *International Index*. The activity of the United States Senate and the House of Representatives is completely indexed in the *Congressional Record*. Some learned information can be secured by investigating the *Agricultural Index, Applied Science and Technology Index, Educational Index, Psychological Index, Psychological Abstracts, Social Science Abstracts*, and *The Monthly Catalog—United States Government Publications*.

Reference Books

Most of us are familiar with the practice of starting our research by turning to the encyclopedia. However, the task of investigation must not stop there; the sincere communicator makes use of other reference materials.

The World Almanac, The Statesman's Year Book, Information Please Almanac, Statistical Abstract of the United States, and Commerce Reports all furnish facts and figures that the speaker may find useful.

Literary references can be found in such books as *Bartlett's Familiar Quotations, Oxford Dictionary of Quotations,* and *The Home Book of Quotations.*

For information about people it is always beneficial to look at some biographical guides. Some of the more useful guides are *Current Biography, Dictionary of American Biography, Who's Who, Who's Who in America, Webster's Biographical Dictionary,* and *International Who's Who.*

Newspapers

Information on almost any topic can be secured from newspapers. While books normally take years to be written and published, newspapers are an excellent source of current happenings and information. Some of the leading newspapers are the *New York Times, Christian Science Monitor, Washington (D.C.) Star, St. Louis Post Dispatch* and the *Los Angeles Times.* Two highly regarded foreign newspapers are the *London Times* and the *Manchester Guardian.* Students with speech topics limited to regional problems and issues will find it helpful to consult the local newspapers.

Magazines and Pamphlets

There are hundreds of magazines available in the United States, and it would be impossible to list all of them. However, there are some current publications which often contain articles on a wide range of subjects: *Time, Newsweek, United States News and World Report, Business Week, Fortune, Life, Look, New Republic, Reporter, Nation, Atlantic Monthly, Commonweal, Harper's Magazine, Current History, National Geographic, Atlas, Foreign Affairs, Yale Review,* and *Vital Speeches of the Day.*

Most libraries also have a large collection of pamphlets that are hard to catalogue and index because of their size and subject. These pamphlets, which are printed and circulated by various groups and organizations such as the American Medical Association and the Automobile Club, cover a wide range of topics. Normally this material can be secured from the library's "vertical file" or by asking the librarian the location of the college's pamphlet collection.

Academic Journals

In addition to the countless magazines written for the layman there are also hundreds of very specialized journals written for very specific audiences. There will be times when it will be helpful to consult one of these academic journals in preparing a speech. Scholarly journals are found in all areas and fields. Whether the topic be education, political science, sociology, speech, home economics, or engineering, there are academic publications available. Ask any library assistant to help you locate the specific journal related to the field you are investigating.

DETECTING FALLACIES

Thus far in this chapter we have stressed three closely related principles: a good speaker includes sufficient evidence to support his position; he tests that evidence to see that it is valid and reliable; he does some serious research and investigation to supplement his ideas. However, simply locating and employing evidence and material is not enough, for the use the speaker makes of this material is as important as the material itself. In short, the speaker's reasoning, as he makes use of his ideas and information, must be clear and free from fallacies in reasoning.

Since communication is concerned with the processes of sending and receiving messages, the thorough student must be alert to mistaken arguments, faulty reasoning, and irrelevant evidence. The examination of evidence, reasoning and ideas for weaknesses is a search for fallacies. Over one hundred years ago Richard Whately, a noted logician, classified as a fallacy "any unsound mode of arguing which appears to demand our conviction, and to be decisive of the question in hand, when in fairness it is not." Not only will a knowledge of some common fallacies serve as a guide to what to avoid, but an awareness of fallacies will enable you to check the remarks and reasoning of others. The communication of the market place is more often than not unsound, and correct reasoning is all too rare. Being cognizant of some of the common types of mistakes in reasoning will let you work on self-correction while at the same time building your defenses against the sophistry of others.

Logicians, social psychologists, and rhetoricians have made repeated attempts at classifying the different types of fallacies, but experience has shown that a satisfactory hard-and-fast division of them has not yet been found. Not only is there a problem of classification and division, but there is also the question of what to include and what to exclude. Discussions of fallacies often contain lists with as many as fifty-one specific kinds of fallacies. In the course of talking about propaganda (Chapter I) and listening (Chapter III) we have mentioned some of the more common types of errors in reasoning and evidence. What is included now is a partial list of some other fallacies with which the student of communication should be familiar.

Ambiguity

Whenever in a speech or conversation the words or phrases being used are ambiguous or are used in an incorrect sense, they may, if unexplained, produce confusion. We know that many words have a large range of meanings, and if the meaning intended by the speaker is not clear, the listener must impose a meaning of his own, which, in turn, may not be the correct interpretation. Frequently ambiguity stems from inadequate definitions, hasty word choice, or loaded language. In each of these instances the words and phrases involved may be interpreted and defined in two or more ways.

In speaking and listening be ever vigilant for words and phrases that are intangible and abstract. "Is a liberal arts education worthwhile?" "Is liberty worth the price?" "Economic democracy is desirable for all of us Americans." "Various races of humanity have not progressed during the last few decades." "Sports are essential for a healthy mind and body." If you look carefully you will discover that each of these statements is meaningless as long as clear and precise definitions are lacking. Verbal disputes can also occur over a single word. Notice the lack of meaning for words such as "justice," "religion," "conservative," "liberal," "communist," "democracy," "extremism," and "happiness."

Ambiguity and other language problems will be discussed in more detail when we consider the use of language in speech (Chapter VIII). But for now let the communicator try to remember to avoid ambiguous words and phrases, define the words he feels to be vague, and establish limits and qualifications for his use of a word.

Hasty Generalization

Snap judgments, jumping to conclusions, or generalizations based on insufficient evidence or experience are all examples of the hasty generalization fallacy. In this fallacy the error is committed because the speaker draws a universal conclusion from evidence which warrants only a restricted conclusion. If you were to meet a Mexican boy and find him lazy, and from this meeting conclude that all Mexicans are lazy, you would be guilty of a hasty generalization.

This fallacy is very common in daily life. Most of us can recall instances in which travelers have experienced one or two unpleasant situations and then reached conclusions concerning the honesty and character of the people in that particular city. Or the example of the person who will not take Professor Smith for history because he knows two students who received D's from Smith. Still another example is the speaker who concluded that all supporters of President Johnson were communists. She said, "Eric Foresman supported Johnson and he is a communist; Scott Allen supported Johnson and he, too, is a communist. So, you see that all supporters of Johnson are communists." And how often we hear people say, "Artists are immoral," "All Republicans are Conservatives," "German Shepherds are mean and vicious," only to discover later that these same people know very few artists, Republicans or German Shepherds.

We mentioned some ways to guard against this fallacy earlier in this chapter when we looked at ways of testing the example and the illustration. It might be wise to return to that section and notice how one can use some of those same techniques to detect the generalization that is irrelevant and based on an isolated case.

Begging the Question

The fallacy of begging the question occurs in several forms, but in every one of its compositions it is committed by assuming at the onset of the argument the very point which is to be established in the conclusion. That is, in this fallacy the speaker assumes the truth or falsity of a statement without proof. If someone in a speech were to state, "Cheating among our students is widespread and bad, and should therefore be abolished," he would be begging the question. In this example the speaker is taking for granted that cheating exists, when in essence the statement can't justify such a conclusion.

Begging the question normally appears in the form of "arguing in a circle." When one proposition is used to prove another proposition we are engaging in this fallacy. An example of arguing in a circle would usually appear in the following form: "Medical Plan X is best because the experts say so. How do we know who the experts are? They are the people who prefer Medical Plan X." In this case begging the question is illustrated by taking as a premise what is true only if the conclusion has been granted to be correct.

Non Sequitur

In a broad sense, any argument which fails to establish its conclusion may be said to be a NON SEQUITUR, for the meaning of the term is simply, "It does not follow." In a more specific sense, however, the fallacy of NON SEQUITUR means that a conclusion is drawn from premises which provide no adequate logical ground for it, or which have no relevant connection with it. "Jones is a good husband and a fine father, so he ought to be elected mayor." It is quite obvious in this example that a logical cause-effect relationship can not be made. Still other statements point out how speakers often reach false conclusions as they try to establish cause-effect connections. "Since only a few people have the ability to handle the complex problems of industry, the wealth and power of this country rightfully belongs in the hands of the rich." "The child is unhappy, beautiful and a college freshman; she must therefore come from an average American family."

One of the most common and insidious forms of this fallacy is POST HOC, ERGO PROPTER HOC, or "after this, therefore because of this." This fallacy manifests itself in assuming that because one occurrence *precedes another in time*, the one is the *cause* of the other. Superstitions belong here. If you walk under a ladder on your way to class and receive an "A" that same day, and then conclude that walking under the ladder gives "A's," you are guilty of POST HOC ERGO PROPTER HOC. Recently a speaker noted, "Since Negroes have been given more educational opportunity we have had an increase in the crime rate throughout the United States. I would conclude, therefore, that the growth in crime is directly related to education." Here again it is just not sufficient to say there is a connection simply because one thing followed the other. In short, because two things happen in sequence does not mean that they are logically or causally connected.

Non-Rational and Irrelevant Evidence

The use of non-rational and irrelevant material is one of the greatest causes for errors in our reasoning. We have already pointed out that many of these problems were discussed in Chapter I when we mentioned the techniques and devices employed by the propagandist. However, these fallacies are so prevalent that they warrant further examination. The most common types of non-rational evidence are: (1) appeals to the emotions and prejudices, (2) appeals to tradition and authority, and (3) appeals to personalities rather than issues.

Appealing only to the emotions and prejudices of the audience, often called ARGUMENTUM AD POPULUM, is a common technique of the speaker who prefers to deal exclusively with the passions of his audience than talk about the salient issues. Instead of presenting empirical evidence and logical argument, the AD POPULUM speaker attempts to win support with phrases such as, "Jewish parasites," "slaughtered women and children," "un-American traitor," "Catholic demagogue," and "friend of the communists." Fortunately, appeals to passions and prejudices become less successful as we become more educated. Yet we must be alert at all times so that we will be able to separate the essential from the non-essential.

A second fallacy, often called ARGUMENTUM AD VERCUNDIAM, shows itself when the speaker offers proof for his position by making an appeal to authority, to a "name," or to an institution. If the authority is legitimately connected to the subject, as Justice White is to the Supreme Court, we have a valid use of expert opinion. However, the fallacy occurs if the appeal is made to justify an authority who is out of his domain or an authority who is unreliable. For example, "George Washington, the Father of our country, warned us against the danger of foreign alliances. Therefore, we should withdraw from the North Atlantic Treaty Organization." It is agreed that Washington was an influential figure during the early history of the United States, but the needs of modern foreign affairs are quite different from the needs expressed in Washington's era. The best defense against the AD VERCUNDIAM fallacy is the use of the tests of authority discussed earlier in the chapter.

In the ARGUMENTUM AD HOMINEM fallacy the speaker attacks someone's character instead of dealing with the relevant issues at hand. That is, the arguments are transferred from principles to personalities. A speaker is engaging in an AD HOMINEM argument when he states, "The city's new highway program should be vetoed. The highway commissioner is a notorious trouble maker and a former lobbyist." Still another case is the speaker that notes, "How can Governor Rockefeller help the poor; he has never been cold or hungry and has been divorced." Notice that in both of these instances the merits of the point at issue are disregarded while attention is focused upon the source. The best defense against this approach is to demand that the person speaking, whether yourself or someone else, stay on the topic and include only material that obviously is relevant.

SUMMARY

In this chapter we have been concerned with four factors of communication that directly affect one another—evidence, the testing of evidence, locating material and detecting fallacies.

The forms of support treated in this chapter represent the fundamental devices used in most types of public discourse and in most private communication situations. These forms are: the detailed factual illustration, the undeveloped illustration (specific instance), the hypothetical illustration, statistics, testimony, analogy and visual aids.

Evidence must meet certain standards if it is to be clear, persuasive and effective. In his book *Argumentation and Debate*, Austin J. Freeley sets forth an excellent summary for testing evidence. His interpretation, in addition to the specific tests discussed in this chapter, should always be considered in using forms of support.

Testing evidence

(1) Is there sufficient evidence? (2) Is the evidence clear? (3) Is the evidence consistent with other known evidence? (4) Can the evidence be verified? (5) Does the evidence come from a competent source? (6) Does the evidence come from an unprejudiced source? (7) Does the evidence come from a reliable source? (8) Is the evidence relevant to the problem? (9) Is the evidence statistically sound? (10) Is it the most recent evidence?

In his search for material the speaker can use his personal experiences and observation, can conduct interviews, can consult indexes, and use newspapers and pamphlets, magazines and academic journals.

One must, in addition to finding evidence, use the forms of support in a sound and logical manner. In thinking straight the speaker, as well as the listener, should be alert to certain fallacies. The most common errors in reasoning and using evidence are ambiguity, hasty generalization, begging the question, NON SEQUITUR, irrational and irrelevant evidence.

SUGGESTED READINGS

ELTON ABERNATHY, *The Advocate: A Manual of Persuasion*, (New York: David McKay Co., Inc., 1964) Chapter 3.

ELLA VIRGINIA ALDRICH, *Using Books and Libraries*, (Englewood Cliffs, N. J.: Prentice-Hall, Inc., 1960).

MARTIN P. ANDERSEN, WESLEY LEWIS, and JAMES MURRAY, *The Speaker and His Audience*, (New York: Harper, 1964). Chapter 10.

MAX BLACK, *Critical Thinking*, 2nd Edition, (New York: Prentice-Hall, Inc., 1952). Chapters 10 and 12.

GLENN R. CAPP, *How to Communicate Orally*, (Englewood Cliffs, N. J.: Prentice-Hall, 1961). Chapters 6 and 7.

W. WARD FEARNSIDE, and WILLIAM B. HOLTHER, *Fallacy: The Counterfeit of Argument*, (Englewood Cliffs, N. J.: Prentice-Hall, Inc., 1959).

AUSTIN J. FREELY, *Argumentation and Debate: Rational Decision Making*, (Belmont, Calif.: Wadsworth Publishing Company, Inc., 1961).

HORACE G. RAHSKOPH, *Basic Speech Improvement*, (New York: Harper and Row, 1965). Chapter 6.

RAYMOND S. ROSS, *Speech Communication, Fundamentals and Practice*, (Englewood Cliffs, N. J.: Prentice-Hall, Inc., 1965). Chapter 10.

VI

ASSEMBLING
THE MESSAGE

ORGANIZATION

Preceding chapters have dealt with those aspects of speech preparation which involve selecting a topic, finding and evaluating material, and determining both the general purpose and the specific purpose of the speech in light of what we know about our audience. With purposes fixed and materials collected we are ready to commence the task of assembling the speech. While there are various ways of approaching this task, we shall concentrate upon the method which involves:

1. Formulating a core statement which expresses the central idea of the speech.

2. Formulating main points to support the core statement (and sub-points to support the main points, if needed).

3. Grouping main points, sub-points, and supporting materials according to consistent patterns of relationship.

4. Ordering main points, sub-points, and supporting materials into a sequence which can effectively develop the core statement.

5. Formulating an introduction.

6. Formulating a conclusion.

It has probably become evident to you that our approach presumes the traditional three-fold division of the speech into introduction, body, and conclusion. While not all speech situations require this formal division, it is workable in the great majority of cases.

THE CORE STATEMENT

The simplest form of speech has essentially two ingredients: (1) a statement or point that requires clarification, amplification or proof, and (2) the materials which clarify, amplify or prove it. A complex speech is simply a combination of such units revolving around an even more general statement. The most general statement of the speech we shall call the CORE STATEMENT; the less general statements we shall call the MAIN POINTS; the least general statements we shall call SUB-POINTS. We may visualize the levels of generality as follows:

Core statement: Our college library is the best library in the state.

Main point: I. It has the best equipment.

Sub point: A. It has the best micro-filming equipment.

Support: 1. A survey taken by the American Library Association shows our equipment is the most up-to-date and the most efficient micro-filming equipment available.

                 2. Edward North, head librarian at the University Library, noted that the college library has just received the best micro-filming equipment in the entire state.

       B. It has the finest study rooms.

           1. Each of the library study rooms has complete air conditioning.

            2. Each of the study rooms is equipped with comfortable seating.

      II. Etc.

The core statement is called by some authors the subject sentence, the theme sentence, the thesis, or the proposition. Whatever the label used, it signifies that element which unifies everything in the speech.

The core statement in a persuasive speech may take the form of a value judgement, such as, "Legal abortion is just as immoral as illegal abortion." It may take the form of a statement of alleged fact, as, "Our foreign aid policy has won us friends around the world." Or it may be worded as a position of policy, such as, "The United States should withdraw from the Organization of American States." In an informative speech it might suggest the steps in a process, "Tiling your kitchen floor involves preparing the underlayment, spreading the mastic, and placing the tiles." It might suggest the parts of a whole, "A modern high fidelity system includes an amplifier, a tuner, a record player, a tape deck, and a set of loudspeakers." Or it might indicate the characteristics which distinguish the subject from other closely related subjects, as in this definition of common law: "Common law is the unwritten law that receives its binding force from immemorial usage and universal reception."

The principal benefit to be derived from formulating the core statement at the outset of the organizational process is that it will provide you with an immediate test of the relevance of any material you expect to introduce in the speech. If any main point, sub point, or supporting material does not clearly relate to the core sentence, then it should be discarded as irrelevant. *Thus the core statement helps insure the unity of the speech.*

It is entirely possible that the core statement may not be spoken during the speech, but it should be implicit in the way in which the speech unfolds. If it is spoken during the speech, it may occur in the opening statement of the introduction, at the start of the body or development of the speech, or at the end of the speech. Whether it should be spoken and when it should be spoken cannot be prescribed by rule. Your careful analysis of the audience should afford you a clue. Remember, one of its functions is to keep you from introducing into the speech materials that are irrelevant and hence confusing to the listener.

FORMULATING MAIN POINTS AND SUB-POINTS

Since the core statement is the most general statement of the speech, we must ask: What less-general statements does it suggest? These less-general statements, as we have noted earlier, constitute the main points of the body of the speech.

Selection and phrasing of the main points should be undertaken with the following guidelines in mind: (1) each main point must grow out of the core statement; (2) each main point must be separable from the other main points; (3) main points must possess consistency; (4) collectively, the main points should develop the core statement completely. Let us examine more fully these four guidelines in operation.

1. *Kinship to the core statement.* If a statement is to be labeled a main point, it must directly support the core statement. One quick test of relevance is to place such connectives as "because" and "for" between the core statement and the alleged main point. For example:

> Core Statement: Our foreign aid policy has won us friends around the world,
>
> *for*
>
>   I. It has won us friends in Latin America.
>
>   II. It has won us friends in Africa.
>
>   III. It has won us friends in Asia.
>
>   IV. It has won us friends in Europe.

Which of the following main points does not meet the test of relevancy?

Core Statement: The so-called "Classical" pattern of speech organization is *useful* today.

 I. It can be *used* to fashion speeches on questions of fact.

 II. It can be *applied* to speeches dealing with questions of value.

 III. It can be *traced* to the speeches of early Sicilian rhetors.

2. *Separability from other main points.* Just as brothers and sisters are related (yet separate) components of the family, so main points should be related (yet separate) components of the speech. The *violation* of separability of main points can be seen in this example:

Core Statement: Capital punishment should be abolished.

 I. It is not effective.

 II. It is not a deterrent.

 III. It is not morally justifiable.

It is apparent that there is overlapping between I and II, inasmuch as the deterrent issue is part of the larger issue of effectiveness. Therefore, II is really a sub-point of I. Or viewed in another light, if effectiveness can be measured only in terms of deterrency, then II is really a restatement of I.

Unless the characteristic of separability is observed in the selection and phrasing of main points, the listener is likely to become very confused.

3. *Consistency of main points.* Maine, California, and Georgia may be regarded as consistent with one another if we are discussing statehood. City, county, state, and nation may be regarded as consistent with one another if we are discussing levels of government. Trains, busses, and planes may be regarded as consistent with one another if we are discussing public transportation.

Where do you detect *inconsistency* in the following?

Core Statement: The hot dog is a national favorite.

 I. It is popular in the West.

 II. It is popular in the East.

III. It is popular in New York.

IV. It is popular in the South.

The foregoing represents not only a violation of consistency of pattern but also a violation of separability. "New York" breaks the pattern of direction and is not separable from "the East."

We shall have more to say of consistency of main points when we turn to the next section of this chapter.

4. _Collective completeness of main points._ We have not discovered all of the main points of a speech if there is a facet of the core statement that has not been developed. We don't think of a family as being complete unless we have all the children and both parents. The mainland visitor to Hawaii often makes the mistake of alluding to matters "back in the States," only to be reminded by the islander that he _is in_ the States. If he ever makes a generalization about the United States without taking Hawaii into account he is quickly corrected.

Determining all of the essential constituents is not always easy. The salesman who wants to convince the customer that his automobile is the best one to buy has to determine the essential constituents of "best," not from his own vantage point, but from what he feels is the vantage point of the customer. To the customer the "best" car might be the most stylish or the most economical to operate or the most powerful. So it is necessary for you to look at your core statement from the vantage point of the listener and ask, "What points will the speaker have to cover before I agree with him?" or "What points will the speaker have to clarify before I understand him?"

Although our discussion in this section has centered around the selection and phrasing of main points, all of the principles brought out are equally applicable to the selection and phrasing of sub-points, since the sub-point bears the same relationship to the main point as the main point bears to the core statement.

GROUPING THE COMPONENTS

Do you remember the first time you ever put together a jig-saw puzzle? If so, you probably recall the initial feeling of frustration in seeing a whole pile of seemingly unrelated parts. Then frustration turned to comprehension when you managed to get several pieces together and could see a design emerging.

Unfortunately, the listener to a speech may not have the patience or incentive to piece together seemingly unrelated bits of information provided by a poorly organized speaker. The listener wants the pattern to emerge at the very outset.

The grouping of main points, sub-points, and supporting materials into consistent patterns of relationship benefits the speaker and the listener. Grouping helps the speaker to recall his ideas more readily and it helps the listener to understand those ideas more readily. In this section we shall discuss three of the most common patterns: (1) chronological arrangement, (2) spatial arrangement, and (3) topical arrangement.

Chronological Arrangement

Certain subjects lend themselves ideally to development in terms of a time sequence. For example, if we wished to discuss the evolution of sound-recording techniques, we would undoubtedly start with the earliest, most rudimentary devices and then move forward in time to the present. Our main points might appear as follows:

Core Statement: The History of sound recording spans more than three-quarters of a century.

Main point: I. The cylinder phonograph was developed in the 1870's.

Main point: II. The disk phonograph was developed in the 1880's.

Main point: III. Sound-on-film recording was developed in the 1920's.

Main point: IV. The wire recorder was developed during the 1930's.

Main point: V. The tape recorder was developed
                        during the 1940's.

Each of these main points, in turn, might be broken down
into a series of sub-points organized chronologically.

The step-by-step method used in describing a process or
in offering instructions is a variation of chronological arrangement. In discussing what happens to a letter from the time
it is mailed until it is received we might arrange our points
accordingly:

Core Statement: Mail handling involves collection, sorting,
                and distribution.

      I. The first step is mail collection.

    II. The second step is primary sorting.

  III. The third step is final sorting.

  IV. The fourth step is primary distribution.

    V. The fifth step is final distribution.

Instructions in changing a tire might include these steps: (1)
laying out the proper tools, (2) jacking up the car, (3) re-
moving the flat tire, (4) putting on the spare tire, and (5)
letting the jack down.

It is generally advisable to keep the number of main points
in a chronological pattern as few as possible—ideally, between
three and five—so that they can be easily retained by the
speaker and easily followed by the hearer. This necessitates
placing a number of chronological details under such general
groupings as "The first era was . . .," "The first decade was
characterized by . . .," or "The ancient Greeks were the first
to systematize the study of public speaking."

Spatial Arrangement

The way in which a series of items relate to one another
in terms of their placement in space affords the speaker an
effective organizational device. In describing a building, you
might arrange the details from basement floor to top floor,
from East wing to West wing, from entrance to exit, from
front to rear. For example:

Core Statement: Each floor of the new Union Building has a special purpose.

    I. The ground floor features shops and restaurants.

    II. The second level features recreational facilities.

    III. The third level features student offices and meeting rooms.

The location of a new stadium might be visualized by employing the spatial pattern:

Core Statement: The new stadium is readily accessible from all parts of town.

    I. Residents from the South Bay area have a choice of three routes.

    II. Residents from the North Bay area have a choice of two routes.

    III. Residents from the inland area have five main arteries from which to choose.

    IV. Residents from the Beaches have the new freeway.

Other topics can best be discussed in terms of a geographical distribution. In giving a picture of our Peace Corps program one could divide the discussion as follows:

Core Statement: The Peace Corps program extends to far-flung places.

    I. Large contingents are to be found in Latin America.

    II. Numerous units are operating in Africa.

    III. Large numbers are to be found in Southeast Asia.

It is possible to combine spatial arrangement with chronological arrangement in discussing certain topics.

Core Statement: That Southern dish, the hushpuppy, has become a national favorite.

    I. The hushpuppy originated in the ante-bellum South.

    II. After the Civil War, Union soldiers took the hushpuppy into the Northern States.

    III. After World War II, the hushpuppy migrated West.

Topical Arrangement

For that vast number of subjects that do not admit of chronological or spatial treatment a much more general mode of arrangement is available. This we call the component-parts or topical mode of arrangement. Many subjects can be broken down into what we would call their "natural divisions." A few examples may illustrate the variety of speech subjects that can be treated topically.

Core Statement: The good leader combines four basic qualities.

    I. He is intelligent.

    II. He is decisive.

    III. He is emotionally mature.

    IV. He is compassionate.

Core Statement: The structure of government proposed for the Republic of Mawandru resembles that of the United States.

    I. Mawandru will have a legislative branch.

    II. It will have a judicial branch.

    III. It will have an executive branch.

Core Statement: The new store features a variety of departments.

    I. It has the West's largest clothing department.

II. It has an excellent appliance department.
III. It has a complete automotive service
department.
IV. It has a fully-stocked grocery.

Core Statement: The fuel selected for manned space ve-
hicles must meet three criteria.
I. It must be safe.
II. It must be efficient.
III. It must be light in weight.

In persuasive speeches the topical arrangement often appears as a series of causes or a series of effects. For example,
if the speaker wants to argue that a given policy will have
dire consequences, he will be proceeding from what he feels
is a known "cause" (the policy) to probable effects. The following example illustrates this mode of arrangement:

Core Statement: U.S. withdrawal from the United Nations
would have serious consequences.
I. There would be serious economic consequences.
II. There would be serious political consequences.
III. There would be serious military consequences.

(The preceding example actually illustrates two sets of natural
divisions—one is the division according to effects, the other is
the familiar division into economic, political and military components.) If the speaker wants to assign causes for some present
condition, he is proceeding from a known effect (the present
condition) to probable causes. The prosecution's case in a
criminal trial affords an illustration:

Core Statement: The defendant (probably) committed the
crime.

    I. He had a motive.

   II. He had a weapon.

  III. He had an opportunity.

In this instance, the circumstances pointing to guilt—the factors of causation—constitute the topics or "natural divisions" of the subject.

We should note at this point that a topical arrangement involving a causal relationship is by no means limited to persuasive speaking. Frequently it can be found in informational speeches as well. A speech explaining trends in modern music might be built around a series of influencing factors.

Speeches concerned with problem-solving also may utilize the topical mode of arrangement. The topics in this case may grow out of (1) presentation of the problem area, (2) presentation of solution, (3) defense of solution. An example of this application of topical arrangement follows:

Core Statement: A bridge should be built from the mainland to the island.

    I. The ferry is an unsatisfactory means of commuting between the mainland and the island.

      A. It is costly.
        (support)

      B. It is inconvenient.
        (support)

      C. It is dangerous.
        (support)

   II. A bridge would represent a solution to the commuting problem.

      A. It would be less expensive.
        (support)

      B. It would be convenient.
        (support)

      C. It would be safe.
        (support)

III. It would be practical to build a bridge.
   A. It would be practical from an engineering standpoint.
      (support)
   B. It would be practical from a financial standpoint.
      (support)
IV. The disadvantages a bridge would bring are minor compared to the advantages.
   A. Residents who would be displaced by construction of bridge-approaches are few.
      (support)
   B. Displaced ferry employees could find employment locally.
      (support)
V. A bridge would be the best solution.
   A. It would be less costly to build than a tunnel.
      (support)
   B. It would not present a navigational hazard as would a causeway.
      (support)
   C. It would be more aesthetically pleasing than a tunnel or a causeway.
      (support)

You will note that both main heads and sub-heads are arranged topically. The main heads involve the topics of problem, solution, and defense of solution. The sub-heads involve several groups of topics. In I and II the sub-heads utilize the topics of cost, convenience, and safety. In III they utilize the topics of engineering feasibility and financial feasibility. In IV the sub-heads are displaced residents and displaced ferry employees. And in V the sub-heads are cost, safety, and beauty. (Note: a truly complete outline would specify in detail the supporting materials to be employed, such as illustrations, specific instances, statistics, testimony, and analogy.)

In the course of a single speech it is possible that all three of the patterns we have discussed can be employed. The main heads, for example, might follow a topical pattern, the sub-heads developing a given main point might follow a spatial pattern, and the supporting materials under a given sub-head might be arranged in a chronological pattern. An expansion of the patterns just discussed, and some additional patterns, will be seen in detail when we approach the processes of informing (Chapter 10).

ORDERING THE COMPONENTS

After main heads, sub-heads, and supporting materials have been placed into consistent groups, the next step is to determine in what order they should be presented so as to support the core statement most effectively. Here again, knowledge of your audience is extremely vital. The attitude which they entertain toward your topic, your purpose, and toward you will be the principal determinant of the order in which you should present your ideas.

In this section we shall suggest some of the more common sequences that are employed, although our list is by no means exhaustive. Some overlapping will be evident.

1. *Proceeding from general to specific.* This sequence is also called the deductive order and is particularly useful in speeches of explanation. For example, if a government worker wanted his listener to visualize his job within the total context of government, he might proceed as follows:

> Department of the Navy
> Bureau of Yards and Docks
> Regional Supply Depot
> Accounting Office

2. _Proceeding from specific to general_. Also known as the inductive order, this sequence finds widespread application in persuasion. If the speaker knows that the announcement of his thesis at the outset would erect barriers to belief, he might begin by presenting items of data which lead to minor conclusions (sub-points) which in turn lead to major conclusions (main points) which in turn lead to the proposition (core statement).

3. _Proceeding from most acceptable to least acceptable_. This order of development is also very useful in persuasion. The speaker will start with those ideas which he feels the audience will most readily accept and moves then to an idea not quite so acceptable (and spending more time in developing it as a consequence) until he reaches the point of greatest resistance.

4. _Proceeding from the easiest to the hardest_. Speeches of explanation frequently are constructed in this sequence. Certainly learning theory is based solidly upon the progression from easiest principles to hardest principles.

5. _Proceeding from past to present or present to past_. We should distinguish between _grouping_ ideas into units of time and _ordering_ ideas chronologically. A time grouping might be:

> Civil War Period
> Post World War II Period   NO SEQUENCE EVIDENT
> Pre-Revolutionary Period

A chronological order would be:

> Pre-Revolutionary Period
> Civil War Period   FORWARD IN TIME
> Post World War II Period
>   or
> Post World War II Period
> Civil War Period   BACKWARD IN TIME
> Pre-Revolutionary Period

6. _Proceeding from one location to another_. Spatially grouped components are more understandable when presented

in a meaningful sequence. If we are going to describe a building, we will be working with spatial components such as top floor, basement, front, rear, north side, south side, and so on. The clarity with which the listener is able to reconstruct the visual details we present depends heavily upon the order in which we present them. If we try to describe the building by starting at the 4th story, then jumping to the 6th story, then down to the 1st story, we succeed only in confusing the listener.

PREPARING THE INTRODUCTION

Once the development of the core statement is carefully plotted, the body of the speech should be complete. The speaker can now turn his attention to fashioning a suitable beginning and ending for the speech. Which of these you will attend to first is a matter of personal preference. The circumstances of your particular communication situation will probably suggest the priority that should be followed. For purposes of our discussion here, we shall deal first with the introduction to the speech.

An examination of representative speeches to inform and persuade will reveal that the introduction to any speech should accomplish two basic purposes: (1) it should get the attention of the audience, and (2) it should prepare the audience for what is to follow. Unless the first purpose is achieved all of the speaker's efforts are for naught. Unless the second purpose is achieved, the speaker risks failure in the accomplishment of his goal.

Gaining Attention

What percentage of the introduction should be devoted to getting the audience's attention? The answer must be, unfortunately, "It all depends." Perhaps the audience is waiting expectantly for the speaker. The mere act of his appearing on the platform may gain attention. On the other hand, his speech may face the stiffest sort of competition for the audience's attention. Perhaps the audience is more concerned with the discomfort of sitting in a hot, stuffy room. Perhaps members of the audience are engaged in animated conversation. Perhaps the speaker faces the kind of captive audience found in required speech classes!

While it would be impossible to catalogue all of the possible ways of opening a speech in an attention-compelling fashion, the following devices are among the most commonly employed. No one device can be regarded as universally applicable. Your choice will ultimately be governed by your subject, your purpose, and your audience.

The Quotation

A thought-provoking or curiosity-arousing quotation can be an effective device for opening many speeches. For example, if you wished to discuss reasons why your listeners should study public speaking, you might utilize this opening:

> "If it is a disgrace to a man when he cannot defend himself in a bodily way, it would be odd not to think him disgraced when he cannot defend himself with reason." This contemporary-sounding piece of advice was offered by Aristotle almost 25 centuries ago when he wrote perhaps the most famous speech text ever, *The Rhetoric*.

A speaker who discussed the relative longevity of men and women opened his speech with this quotation:

> "The stronger sex is actually the weaker sex because of the weakness of the stronger sex for the weaker sex." This humorous observation noted in the evening newspaper just yesterday has more truth to it than appears at first glance.

The important criteria to use in selecting a quotation for an opening are *relevancy, provocativeness,* and *good taste.* A quotation cited simply to gain attention and nothing more is apt to create ill-will when it becomes obvious to the listener that the device bears no connection to the speaker's subject. The quotation that is not provocative simply fails in its task of eliciting audience attention. Finally, the quotation which is in poor taste will certainly get the audience's attention, but it is apt to be the kind of attention that militates against the accomplishment of the speaker's purpose!

The Illustration or Story

Among the most familiar devices for opening speeches are stories or illustrations. When properly handled they can be perhaps the most effective openings of all, because interesting narratives tend to cause the listener to attend effortlessly. On the other hand, tired stories that the audience has heard innumerable times in the past can "turn off" audience attention. Before using this familiar opening device the speaker should make certain (1) that the story or illustration is fresh (old stories told from a new slant are as fresh as brand-new stories), (2) that it is pertinent to the main theme of the speech, (3) that it can be effectively related by the speaker (any limitations as a story teller should be considered), and (4) that it be in good taste. This last quality cannot be stressed too much, especially if the story is a humorous one. The speaker must be extremely thorough in his audience analysis to ferret out any information that would alert him to issues of taste. As a general rule it is wise to avoid stories that derive their humor from ridicule of religion or racial origin. Self-directed ridicule is perhaps the safest form of humor to employ in the story or illustration. (See our treatment of illustrations in the preceding chapter for additional guidelines.)

The Rhetorical Question

A skillfully phrased question that puts the audience into a state of expectancy for an answer is a very effective means of gaining attention. But let us call attention to that important qualification—*that puts the audience in a state of expectancy for an answer.* Without this qualification, the rhetorical question is ineffectual as an attention device. Of course, what it is that puts an audience into a state of expectancy will differ from audience to audience. A group of entering freshmen would have their attention piqued by hearing the Dean of Admissions use this rhetorical question at an orientation meeting, "How many of you will be here next year to start your sophomore year?"

The question, "Where can you buy a first edition of Blair's *Lectures on Rhetoric and Belles Lettres* for 29 cents?" would probably evoke this reaction from a group of chemistry majors: "I don't know and I don't care to know!" To an audience of graduate students of rhetoric or to a group of dedicated bibliophiles it might well have an electrifying effect. Here again we can see the importance of knowing your audience before you plan your strategy.

The Startling Statement

An audience that is prone to be apathetic toward your topic can often be made attentive by the use of a statement that startles or shocks them. This is particularly true of speeches on familiar themes, such as requests for contributions to charitable organizations, to cancer drives, to heart funds, or speeches exhorting us to exercise our right to vote, or urging us to wear seat belts. The startling statement in such cases might be characterized by a direct reference to a person or persons in the audience. For example, a speaker might begin: "I'm sure that all of you are just as sad as I am that these three gentlemen sitting in the front row are going to have to undergo a lengthy hospitalization which will cause them to use up all their savings, sell their homes, and most of their belongings." Such a statement would certainly get the attention of the "three gentlemen" and would probably rouse the curiosity of the other members of the audience. To be effective, the startling statement, like all attention devices, should be relevant to the topic and should rest upon a thorough understanding of your audience. It is easy to see that indiscriminate use of the startling statement could have a self-defeating effect.

Referring to the Subject

Of all the stock openings this is perhaps the most overworked, and often the most unsuccessful in gaining attention. Its use should be reserved for those subjects in which you are confident your audience is already interested, so that the mere mention of the subject will provoke a high level of interest. If your topic does not possess this inherent interest value for your audience, then avoid this type of opening. To illustrate, we can guess that an audience will be inherently interested in gossipy information about famous public figures. Therefore, we can, with impunity, open with, "Today I'd like to share with you some little known facts about the off-screen behavior of a glamorous movie star." We can also guess that an audience will not be inherently interested in an explanation of some esoteric subject. Thus, "Today I'd like to talk about residual disjunctive enthymemes" will probably produce a yawn from the listener.

If your topic has a high curiosity potential or if it is a topic that people are talking excitedly about before your speech, then a simple reference to the subject may be your quickest way to achieve audience attention. If your topic doesn't have these built-in guarantees of audience interest, then you'd better choose another attention device.

Referring to the Occasion

This device may be very useful on relatively formal speech occasions, such as a banquet, a graduation ceremony, a dedication, a special lecture—in short, in any case where the *occasion* is the dominant factor. In the average speech class, however, such a formal opening would seem "stuffy" and affected, unless it happened to be the first day or the last day of the semester.

Preparing Your Audience
for the Speech

This function of the introduction may be accomplished in a wide variety of ways. What constitutes adequate audience preparation can never be universally prescribed. However, we can describe some of the things that are commonly done; your topic, your purpose, and your analysis of the audience will dictate which of these will be applicable in your case.

Justifying the Topic

In those instances when your audience has not gathered for the express purpose of hearing you talk about a given topic you need to offer them a reason for listening. "So you're going to talk about petroleum distillates. What's in it for me?" may well be the kind of reaction your audience experiences upon the announcement of your topic. Well, what *is* in it for your audience? How do petroleum distillates affect their lives? Will your treatment of the subject benefit the audience in some tangible way? Will it help them make more money, be healthier, be more popular? Will it benefit them in intangible ways? Will it satisfy their sense of curiosity? Will it satisfy their need for emotional expression?

In speeches to inform the justification of the topic answers the question, "Why do I need this information?" In the speech to persuade it answers such questions as "How does this issue affect me?" "Why should I be concerned about this problem and its solution?"

Sometimes the device used for gaining attention can also serve to justify the topic. For example, a rhetorical question may provoke attention and instill a need for information.

It should be remembered that the justification of the topic is not always needed. In many cases the audience will arrive already motivated. For instance, it would be unnecessary to spend time justifying a discussion of proposed pay raises before an audience of college professors who would be the recipients of the salary increase.

Delimiting the Topic

It may be necessary for you to draw the boundaries of your discussion when approaching certain topics. To say "I'm going to discuss marijuana" is to lead the audience to anticipate a number of possibilities. Will you discuss the structure of the marijuana plant, where marijuana is grown, how marijuana is processed, how marijuana affects the user, the evils of marijuana, where marijuana is sold, who uses marijuana, the effects of marijuana versus the effects of alcohol? In such cases it may be well for you to point out not only what you are going to cover but also what you are going to exclude from the discussion. By providing the listeners with the boundaries of your discussion you enable them to adjust their expectations accordingly. It helps them clear their minds of issues that are beside the point of your speech. Furthermore, it gives the audience a certain kind of security to know just how far the speaker intends to go. It will then not be so impatient for those beautiful words, "And in conclusion. . . ."

To be sure, there are occasions when it is unwise to indicate the boundaries of your discussion, especially if the creation of a feeling of suspense is essential to the accomplishment of your purpose. (But be sure this is not a rationalization resulting from confusion in your own mind as to the boundaries of your discussion!)

Presenting Your Credentials to Speak

If your authority to speak on a subject is not known to your audience, it may be necessary for you to establish it in the speech. Normally this would be done for you by the person introducing you to the audience, but if the introducer is derelict in this duty (or if there is no introducer at all), the task falls upon you.

Why should your credentials be made known? Audiences tend to place greater credibility in the remarks of speakers they consider to be "expert." Furthermore, they tend to listen more attentively to the "expert." An older student in a speech class once gave a talk on how pilots landed an airplane by instrument alone. After his talk he was asked by one of his classmates where he had found his information. He replied, "I was a commercial airline pilot for five years." Suddenly his remarks became much more vital to the class, and one student said, "I wish he'd give the speech over again."

What are your credentials? Obviously you cannot always be an "expert" in the sense of being vocationally involved. But that does not mean you cannot speak with authority on a subject. Through reading and research you can so familiarize yourself with a subject that you are an "expert" in comparison with those who are your listeners. Perhaps your authority derives from close association with those who are, in fact, "experts."

How shall you make your credentials known? This can usually be accomplished without creating the impression of immodesty. Here are a few examples:

> "I'd like to share with you some facts about radiation poisoning that I learned in a class in radiological medicine last semester."
>
> "As a 'Navy brat' I've had more 'home towns' than I can remember right off hand. But my favorite home town has always been San Diego. Today I'd like to discuss just what it is that makes San Diego unique."
>
> "In doing a term paper for American history last semester, I became interested in Benedict Arnold's role in the American Revolution. Just how serious were his misdeeds? Was the war effort really hampered? I shall attempt to give you my answers to these questions today."

Defining Terms

If the subject you are discussing involves special terminology, jargon, or "technical talk," it will be advisable for you to offer definitions early in the speech. Perhaps you will set aside a portion of the introduction to define all terms to be used, or perhaps you will define each term when it first appears in the speech.

Providing Background Information

There are occasions when a full appreciation or understanding of a subject cannot be gained unless one is familiar with certain background details. The background materials often are in the form of historical details. To discuss some great event without indicating the historical context in which it occurred is to deny the listener an important dimension for his understanding.

Other background details may be physical in nature. For example, to have an audience sense the grandeur of the Lincoln Memorial one has to put it in its physical context. An architect's genius cannot be fully appreciated by simply examining the building that he has designed. One has to see how it integrates with its physical environment.

Establishing a Common Ground

Not infrequently we are forced into taking an unpopular stand on some controversial issue. If we wish to win audience support for our position, we must pave the way carefully. One of the measures that is often used is the establishment of a common ground of belief with your audience. In essence, this means that you will take pains to stress areas of agreement before turning to those issues on which you and your audience hold divergent viewpoints. It is even conceivable that this act of establishing a common ground may occupy the major share of your speech.

PREPARING THE CONCLUSION

"Well, I guess that's about all. Are there any questions?" This is an all-too-common ending to speeches. Judge for yourself whether it accomplishes the usual functions of a speech conclusion: (1) Does it re-direct the audience's attention to the central point of the speech? (2) Does it usher the listener into the frame of mind that should be dominant at the end? (3) Does it leave the listener with a sense of completeness?

We would hazard the guess that the average speech student gives less thought to preparing his conclusion than he gives to almost any other facet of speech preparation. Yet the conclusion can be the most critical part of the speech. An ineffectual ending can undermine all that has been accomplished by the speaker in the preceding portions of the speech.

Let us examine, then, some of the possible methods of ending a speech effectively.

The Summary

A brief recapitulation of the main points of the speech is a common device used in concluding. It is particularly valuable in instructional speeches, because it reinforces the instructions which the speaker wishes the audience to recall. For example, in concluding a speech on "The Fundamentals of Tennis" a speaker would use the summary in the following manner: "Today, having learned some of elementary techniques of tennis, you should try to remember that (1) your eye should always be kept on the ball, (2) that you should keep your arm firm, and (3) you should remember to follow-through with your swing." In persuasive speeches it can serve to remind the listener that sound reasons have been advanced for the belief the speaker wishes them to hold, or for the action he wishes them to take.

Usually the summary is employed in conjunction with other concluding devices, since by itself it may not accomplish all of the purposes of a conclusion that we noted above.

The Quotation

Just as the quotation can be effectively employed as means of gaining attention at the beginning of a speech, it can be employed to end the speech on a graceful, stimulating note. Sometimes it is possible to use two quotations from the same person, one for a beginning and one for an ending. Or perhaps a repetition of the same quotation used in the opening will be fitting at the end of the speech. Whatever the quotation chosen, it should meet the tests of relevancy, good taste, and impact.

A good example of the effective use of quotation can be seen in General Douglas MacArthur's address to Congress upon being recalled from his command in Korea:

> The world has turned over many times since I took the oath on the plain at West Point, and the hopes and dreams have long since vanished, but I still remember the refrain of one of the most popular barracks ballads of that day which proclaimed most proudly that "old soldiers never die; they just fade away."

The Illustration or Story

Like the quotation, the illustration or story can be used effectively at both extremities of the speech. It is particularly useful as a method of visualizing for the listener the import of what you have been discussing in the body of the speech.

It distills the essence of your message and presents it in a form that makes it memorable to the listener.

If the prevailing mood of your speech has been one of unrelieved seriousness, an illustration or story in a light vein may provide the touch needed to leave the audience in the right frame of mind.

The Challenge

Speeches which are designed to stimulate the audience to greater efforts or stronger devotion to some cause or ideal lend themselves well to this kind of ending. Occasionally an informative speech can employ this ending as well if the speaker wishes the audience to seek information in addition to that which he has just presented in the body of the speech. In any case, the challenge should be worded in such a way as to encourage a spirit of optimism in the audience's attempt to meet the challenge. If the challenge seems impossible of fulfillment, a negative attitude is generated which runs counter to the speaker's intentions.

A good example of the use of the challenge may be seen in Henry George's famous speech, "The Crime of Poverty."

> . . . . I cannot hope to convince you in talking for an hour or two, but I shall be content if I shall put you upon inquiry. Think for yourselves; ask yourselves whether this widespread fact of poverty is not a crime, and a crime for which every one of us, man and woman, who does not do what he or she can do to call attention to it and to do away with it, is responsible.

Declaration of Intent

Speeches intended to induce action can be concluded effectively when the speaker sets an example for the audience by declaring what he personally plans to do. Patrick Henry's famous closing remarks in his "Liberty or Death" speech is perhaps the first example that comes to mind. A less familiar example can be seen in a speech delivered by Daniel Webster in the U. S. Senate when he and Calhoun were debating the nature of the Constitution:

I am ready to perform my own appropriate part, whenever and wherever the occasion may call on me, and to take my chance among those upon whom blows may fall first and fall thickest. I shall exert every faculty I possess in aiding to prevent the Constitution from being nullified, destroyed, or impaired; and even should I see it fall, I will still, with a voice feeble, perhaps, but earnest as ever issued from human lips, and with fidelity and zeal which nothing shall extinguish, call on the People to come to its rescue.

OTHER SPEECH DESIGNS

In this chapter we have discussed organization as it relates to the familiar threefold division of the speech into introduction, body, and conclusion. But we do not wish to suggest that this is the only, or necessarily the best, way to lay out a speech design. In fact, many effective speeches defy reduction into the three familiar divisions. As we have indicated repeatedly, questions of choice in public speaking can be answered only in terms of each individual public speaking situation.

We should like to mention briefly some of the other speech designs with which you should become more familiar after you have mastered the conventional design we have discussed in this chapter.

The Motivated Sequence

Professor Alan H. Monroe in his *Principles and Types of Speech* recommends the division of the persuasive speech into five steps which constitute "The Motivated Sequence": (1) The Attention Step (the label suggests its function); (2) The Need Step (wherein the problem area is exposed); (3) The Satisfaction Step (wherein the solution to the problem is explained); (4) The Visualization Step (wherein the speaker describes conditions as they will be in the future relative to his proposal); and (5) The Action Step (wherein the speaker gives directions for implementing his solution).

The Extended Illustration

This speech design is applicable to both informative and persuasive speeches. A speaker who wishes to explain the duties of a policeman, for example, might build his speech around "a typical day" in the life of a real or hypothetical policeman. By translating his facts into narrative form he utilizes an effective ingredient for keeping audience interest high.

A persuasive speech designed to elicit contributions to the multiple sclerosis fund might be translated into a narrative involving a person who contracts multiple sclerosis and his battle for survival.

The Classical Design

The formal structure employed by orators of the Roman Empire has been found suitable for many speaking situations ever since. The classical design involves six divisions of the speech: (1) The Exordium, which is roughly analogous to the Attention Step of the Motivated Sequence; (2) The Narration, wherein the speaker furnishes background details on the subject; (3) The Partition, or "preview" of the points to be dealt with subsequently; (4) The Proof, wherein the speaker develops his argument; (5) The Refutation, wherein he answers the arguments that have been or could be raised against his argument; (6) The Peroration, which is roughly analogous to what we have called the conclusion.

SUMMARY

The process of assembling the speech usually begins with the formulation of a core statement that embodies the central idea of the speech. Growing out of the core statement are the main points, sub-points, and supporting materials. Coordinate points should (1) be related to the core statement, (2) related to one another yet separable from one another, and (3) collectively they should fully develop the statement under which they stand. Coordinate points should be meaningfully grouped. Among the patterns of grouping are chronological arrangement, spatial arrangement, and topical arrangement. Once grouped, they should be put into a sequence which will most effectively support the core sentence. Among the sequences are movement from general to specific, from specific to general, from most acceptable to least acceptable, from the easiest to the hardest, from past to present or present to past, from one location to another.

After the body of the speech has been designed, the speaker formulates an introduction and a conclusion. An introduction serves to gain attention and prepare the audience for what is to follow. Among the methods of gaining attention are the quotation, the illustration or story, the rhetorical question, the startling statement, the reference to the subject, and the reference to the occasion. Preparing the audience from what is to follow may involve justifying the topic, delimiting the topic, presenting your credentials to speak, defining terms, providing background information, and establishing a common ground.

The conclusion serves to re-direct the audience's attention to the core statement, to usher the audience into the proper frame of mind consistent with the speaker's purpose, and to give the listener a sense of completeness. Some methods of concluding are the summary, the quotation, the illustration or story, the challenge, and the declaration of intent.

In addition to the traditional tri-partite division of speeches into introduction, body and conclusion, there is the motivated sequence, the extended illustration, and the classical design.

SUGGESTED READINGS

VIRGIL L. BAKER, and RALPH T. EUBANKS, *Speech in Personal and Public Affairs*, (New York: David McKay Company, Inc., 1965). Chapters 12-15.

LAWRENCE D. BRENNAN, *Modern Communication Effectiveness*, (Englewood Cliffs, N. J.: Prentice-Hall, 1963). Chapter 11.

DONALD C. BRYANT, and KARL R. WALLACE, *Fundamentals of Public Speaking*, (New York: Appleton-Century-Crofts, Inc., 1953). Chapters 9, 10, 22, 23.

HERBERT L. CARSON, *Steps in Successful Speaking*, (Princeton, N. J.: D. Van Nostrand Co., Inc., 1967). Part II.

S. JUDSON CRANDELL, GERALD M. PHILLIPS, and JOSEPH A. WIGLEY, *Speech: A Course in Fundamentals*, (Chicago: Scott, Foresman and Company, 1963). Chapter 8.

LIONEL CROCKER, and HERBERT W. HILDEBRANDT, *Public Speaking for College Students*, (New York: American Book Company, 1965). Chapter 19.

GILES WILKESON GRAY, and WALDO W. BRADEN, *Public Speaking: Principles and Practice*, (New York: Harper and Row, 1963). Chapter 14.

ROY C. McCALL, and HERMAN COHEN, *Fundamentals of Speech*, 2nd edition, (New York: The Macmillan Company, 1963). Chapter 4 and 5.

ALAN H. MONROE, *Principles and Types of Speech*, (Chicago: Scott, Foresman, 1962). Chapters 14-16.

HORACE G. RAHSKOPF, *Basic Speech Improvement*, (New York: Harper and Row, 1965). Chapter 9.

PAUL L. SOPER, *Basic Public Speaking*, 3rd edition, (New York: Oxford University Press, 1963). Chapter 5.

JAMES A. WINANS, *Speech Making*, (New York: Appleton-Century-Crofts, Inc., 1938). pp. 116-130.

VII

MAKING THE MESSAGE INTERESTING

HOLDING ATTENTION

You have doubtless discovered the importance of listening attentively to lectures and classroom discussions. And certainly you have discovered how difficult that task can be when the speaker seems intent upon boring you to death! His inability to keep you attentive may not stem from a lacklustre delivery. In fact, he may well exemplify all of those qualities of effective delivery we discussed in Chapter IV. His difficulty is to be found in his ideas. They lack that quality which holds interest. So you have to exert all the self-discipline you can muster to get something out of all the tedium. On the other hand, another speaker, using basically the same ideas makes listening an effortless act for you. You listen in spite of yourself! You pay attention.

We might, for our analysis, think of attention and interest as inter-changeable. Admittedly, the dictionary may well offer two different definitions, but when we talk about human behavior, attention and interest have meanings that are interlocking and overlapping. An examination of your own behavior can't help but take you directly to the conclusion that what interests you commands your attention, and what you pay attention to interests you. In this approach to attention and interest we are talking about the manner in which our awareness of a given stimulus is greatly heightened. All competing stimuli are secondary as the main message goes directly to what Psychologist William James called the "focus of consciousness."

We do not pretend to know any magic formula that will transform a dull message into a scintillating experience for the listener. Each speaking situation makes its own unique demands; hence, there could hardly be a universal formula for success. But we can profit from the findings of psychologists who have probed into the nature of attention and interest. These findings have enabled us to devise guidelines for minimizing the effort our listeners will have to exert in order to stay attentive to our ideas. A discussion of some of these guidelines shall be the principal concern of this chapter. Whether your purpose be to inform, entertain, or persuade, we believe that the following guidelines will assist you in finding ways of making your message more interesting.

Tie Your Message to Something Recent

While sitting in the waiting room at your dentist's office have you ever discovered that the only magazine remaining in the rack is a two-year-old copy of a weekly news magazine? Even if you hadn't read it when it was published, you aren't very curious to read it now, because it's "old hat." You are concerned with what is current.

The wise speaker will try to associate his ideas with something recent whenever possible. For example, a speaker who wishes to explain the principles of rocket propulsion might well allude to the recent launching of a space vehicle as reported on television or in the newspaper. Or a person wishing to discuss the alleged deterrent value of capital punishment might first of all allude to a news clipping reporting the latest execution or a recent statement made by the governor regarding his stand on capital punishment. This association of your theme with a recent happening gives a freshness and immediacy to your ideas that tends to make an audience interested in listening further.

Tie Your Message to Something Impending

Not only are we interested in that which has just happened but also in that which is soon to happen. A person who wants to discuss needed improvements in the safety features of automobiles might say, "I heard on the radio this morning that the first of the new model cars are due to hit the dealers' showrooms within the next ten days. It will be interesting to see how they measure up to the safety standards I'd like to discuss with you today."

You have probably noticed how much more interested people become in taxation on the eve of a school bond election. Or how prognostications about the outcome of conference football standings take on greater interest the closer we get to the start of the football season. So look for ways of linking your subject to an event in the immediate future.

Tie Your Message to Something That Is Physically Near to Your Audience

Just as ideas involving temporal nearness tend to catch our interest more readily than those that are in the distant past or distant future, so ideas involving physical proximity tend to be more compelling than those that are remote. A news item that involves your immediate neighborhood probably will capture your attention faster than one concerned with the other side of town.

The speaker has many opportunities to exploit this interest factor. If he were trying to explain the height of an aircraft's tail section, he might compare it to the room or the building in which the audience is situated. If he were discussing the principle of the micro-wave relay of telephone messages, he might say, "Look out the window at the bank building over there. See that large dish-shaped antenna on the roof? That is part of the coastal network of relay stations that enables you to talk to cities 800 miles to the north." Or the speaker who wishes to use a hypothetical illustration to explain some principle of boating safety might say, "Tim and Joan here are going out to Mission Bay this weekend and rent one of those small sailboats for a cruise around the Bay." By giving the audience someone close at home to identify with the audience will likely be more interested in following the illustration. Every teacher soon learns the attention value of a student's name to perk up that person's interest.

Tie Your Message to Something That Is Familiar to Your Audience

A parachutist once remarked, "Jumping out of a plane gives you somewhat the same sensation you experience when you unexpectedly reach the top step of a dark stairway. You raise your foot for another step, then discover it isn't there." By relating the unfamiliar (jumping out of a plane) to the familiar (reaching for a step that isn't there) the speaker enabled his listeners to experience vicariously a small part of his favorite pastime.

This technique of relating the unfamiliar to the familiar is basic to effective speaking whether it be persuasive or informative in character. The listener's frame of reference must always be considered when we attempt to explain a new idea or concept. The use of reference to the familiar, however, does not mean that we simply tell the audience what it already knows. Rather, we tell the audience what it doesn't know in terms of what it does know.

Tie Your Message to Something That Is Vital to the Listener

Who is the most important person in the world to the listener? It's probably the listener himself. And what directly affects him will be of interest to him. Does your message have any bearing upon the listener's self interests? Does it concern, directly or indirectly, his health, his safety, his family, his pocketbook, his status, his personal comforts, or any of a long list of needs, wants, and desires? Every listener may subconsciously be asking the speaker, "What's in it for me?" It is the speaker's responsibility to have an answer ready.

A speech concerning a nuclear power plant might be prefaced by remarks concerning possible cuts in the listener's light bill or new conveniences he is going to enjoy as a result of cheaper electricity. A discussion of U. S. foreign policy takes on added interest when the speaker suggests that the draft status of the men in the audience might be affected by certain proposed policies. An explanation of computer operation may draw closer attention if the speaker alludes to the mate-matching applications of computers. Never overlook the possibility of relating your message to the personal concerns of the audience.

Tie Your Message to Something Active

In our chapter on delivery, we pointed out how the speaker who uses meaningful bodily action and vocal variety tends to hold attention more readily than the speaker who fails to employ them. The content of the speech can also be infused with activity. If the speaker arranges his ideas in a logical, easy-to-follow sequence, those ideas seem to *move* for the listener. A jumbled, helter-skelter lack of arrangement is one of the surest techniques for losing audience interest.

Words which suggest action should be fully employed by the speaker. "He staggered home" is more compelling than "He went home drunk." "His old pick-up truck was doing seventy-five when it drifted over the divider strip into the oncoming lane" is more meaningful and interesting than "He was going too fast in that old truck."

The authors recall a classroom speech on memory improvement in which the speaker demonstrated a technique for memorizing a list of items. Among other things, the speaker asked the audience to visualize each item in motion—the more absurd and exaggerated the motion the better. He explained that we tend to remember moving objects more readily than stationary ones.

Varying your developmental materials also imparts a feeling of activity to your message. Don't dwell too long on sets of statistics; intersperse them with examples, analogies, quotations from authorities. In discussing a serious topic, don't fall into a pattern of unrelieved sobriety. Insert a light note here and there (consistent with your purpose, of course) to lend refreshing variety.

Tie Your Message to Something Unusual

The yearning to be distinctive seems to be a universal desire. A cross-country tour will reveal countless towns and villages, each of which claims title to something unique, such as "The Quilt-Making Center of the United States," "Home of the world's largest feeding pen," "The oldest county seat west of the Mississippi," or some similar claim to fame. Ludicrous as these examples may be, they do illustrate an important avenue of interest. What is unique or novel about the information you would like to impart to your audience? Is the novelty built-in to your subject, as it would be in the case of a speech about flying saucers or head-hunters? Or do you have to search for ways of injecting it, as in the case of a speech about water filtration?

The use of contrast can be an effective method of infusing an element of the unusual into certain ideas. One speaker discussing the Battle of Stalingrad in World War II noted that the Russian losses in that one campaign were greater than the total losses U. S. forces have sustained throughout the history of our nation. Another speaker made the U. S. standard of living more meaningful and interesting by contrasting it with that of some of the vaunted civilizations of the past.

Putting something that is commonplace into an unusual setting can also be a source of interest. One science fiction movie derived its novelty from reducing men to microscopic size for a voyage through a normal-sized man's circulatory system!

Tie Your Message to Something Suspenseful

We are all familiar with the interest value of suspense in drama. Even when we know the hero is going to emerge triumphant in the final scene, we can't help but feel anxiety for his welfare as he meets obstacle after obstacle along the way. Of course, when the final outcome is unpredictable, then the suspense can become even more extreme.

The speaker would do well to emulate the playwright in exploiting suspense as a factor of interest. Starting the speech with a rhetorical question that makes the audience eager for an answer is one application of suspense to speaking. Or a statement that promises a reward if the audience will listen carefully to what is to follow can generate suspense. The problem-solving speech often holds attention by the very fact that it puts the audience into a state of expectancy.

Here are examples from classroom speeches that have generated suspense: "The next five minutes may be the most important five minutes of your life," said one speaker prior to giving instructions on administering heart massage. "If you follow the suggestions I'm about to cite, you'll be two hundred dollars richer by the end of this semester," was the preface to a speech on deceptive food packaging. A discussion of delayed speech revolved around the true story of a child who was assumed to be mentally defective and would have been committed to an institution but for the fortuitous appearance of a speech pathologist upon the scene.

Tie Your Message to Something Concrete

Ideas that evoke sensory responses tend to hold attention more readily than those that are abstract. Thus "a clear, crisp autumn afternoon" is more attention-compelling than "a beautiful day," because it evokes specific images of sight, temperature perception, perhaps the smell of burning leaves, or the sound of a crowded football stadium.

Abstract ideas may be made clear and interesting by translating them into forms that are perceptible to the senses. The metaphor and the simile are stylistic devices often used to accomplish this transformation. Thus permanence is depicted by the Rock of Gibraltar, courage is epitomized by the lion, and stealth is suggested by the cat. One of the best ways to define a term like "democracy" or "honor" is to narrate vividly an event which embodies your conception of the term.

Choosing the specific word or phrase in preference to the general helps you to achieve concreteness. "A battered roll-top desk" is more image-evoking than "old furniture," "El

Paso" can be visualized more readily than "a Southwestern city," "Fidel Castro" is more meaningful than "a dictator."

One speaker made the function of an enzyme more meaningful by asking the audience to visualize the enzyme as a "Marryin' Sam" who brings together two compatible substances and unites them into a new state.

Tie Your Message to Something Real

A policeman explaining his job to a group of students in an evening speech class related what happened to him that very day. He mentioned the fact that he had issued a number of citations for traffic infractions. Reaching in his hip pocket he pulled out a pad of citation forms. "There are twenty blank forms in a full pad. I have one form left in this pad." An accountant explaining his job to that same class said that, among other things, he was responsible for drawing up stockholders' reports. At that point he held up a sheaf of papers, saying, "Here's the annual report for my firm that I just finished drawing up this past weekend." A bank teller explaining how to recognize counterfeit currency asked each listener to take a dollar bill out of his wallet and examine it closely as the speaker explained each clue to look for.

The policeman didn't need to pull out his citation pad in order to make that facet of his job meaningful to the listeners. The accountant didn't need to use his firm's report in order to clarify his work. He could have used a hypothetical example as easily. The bank teller could have drawn a representation of the dollar bill on the board and made his instructions for counterfeit detection just as clear. But in all three cases a striking heightening of interest resulted from the use of an *actual* object. The "real McCoy" is almost always more compelling than the best verbal description, pictorial representation, or mock-up that can be devised. By the same token reference to an actual example tends to be more compelling than reference to a hypothetical example. Our policeman could have manufactured "a typical day," but he wisely chose to relate what happened on "an actual day."

It isn't always possible or practical to produce "the real thing," whether it be an object or an example. In such cases we have to substitute that which is *realistic* for that which is *real*. For example, if we are trying to get our audience to visualize some circumstance in the future we obviously can't produce the actual circumstance. But we can provide *life-like* details that will cause the listener to respond, "Yes, that could very well happen." Putting real people in hypothetical circumstances or hypothetical people into an actual setting lends credibility *and interest* to such examples. You will recall our example of a few pages back where the speaker said, "Tim and Joan here are going out to Mission Bay this weekend and rent one of those small sailboats for a cruise around the Bay." While the event depicted was hypothetical, the people and places were real. Thus the event bore a resemblance to reality.

Tie Your Message to the Human Element

From childhood on we tend to assign human qualities to non-human things, both animate and inanimate. We even transform abstract concepts into human form as witnessed by "Winged Victory" in sculpture. This practice of personifying a thing or a concept seems to stem from a desire to put everything into a human frame of reference—perhaps in order to understand it better or in order to make some adjustment to it. In most cases, investing the non-human thing with human qualities makes it more interesting.

One speaker made the process of water filtration more interesting by adopting a narrative approach in which the central figure was a dirty drop of water. He gave the drop a name, a personality, an environment, and then in the best Walt Disney fashion put "Donald the Drip" into an "adventure." With appropriate imagery he described Donald's anguish at being pulled away from his friends in the lake by the suction of the great intake pump, related his exciting trip through the maze of filters, and his astonishment at the wonderful change in his appearance as he emerged crystal-clear from the water tap.

Advertisers realize the value of associating the human element with products. A refrigerator is pictured being opened by the housewife; a car is shown being driven by a glamorous blonde; a home in a new subdivision is shown fully equipped with a family.

Whether you invest a thing with human traits or give it a human companion is not particularly important. If the human element is there, interest will tend to follow.

Tie Your Message to Something Involving Conflict

Most major collegiate football teams schedule at least one game per season that can be considered "a sure thing," because the opponent is a small school with no reputation for giant-killing or is a large school with a long record of defeats. Gate attendance at such games is apt to be low, with only the most ardent fans showing up. Such a game provokes little interest because there is no prospect of a real contest taking place, hence, no conflict.

For a zestful existence man seems to require some element of struggle or conflict. Perhaps he finds it in his job, in community service, in a hobby, or perhaps vicariously by watching plays or films, reading books, attending sporting events which involve a struggle between opposing forces. But once any of these activities become predictable routine, "sure things," his interest fades.

The speaker should be aware of the value of conflict as a means of holding audience interest on a subject. Perhaps conflict is implicit in the subject itself. A speech opposing a proposed course of action has built-in conflict. A problem-solving speech has built-in conflict. Subjects in which conflict is not implicit, on the other hand, require that the speaker superimpose it. A speech explaining what happens to a letter from the time it is mailed to the time it reaches its destination does not seem to have the element of conflict built-in. But by skillful use of a hypothetical illustration a postal worker did introduce conflict into that subject. He asked the audience to imagine that one of the men in the front row was carrying in his suit pocket an insurance premium he had forgotten to mail. To keep his insurance in effect the premium would have to reach the home office 1200 miles away within 36 hours. Would mailing the premium at this moment enable it to reach the company in time? For the remainder of the speech he followed the progress of that particular piece of mail until, happily, it reached its destination in the nick of time. The twin ingredients of conflict and suspense kept the audience interested throughout the entire speech.

Tie Your Message to Something Humorous

Judicious use of humor can be perhaps the most effective means of holding audience interest. However, its effective employment requires real skill. Because of its unpredictable nature, we would caution you to use it sparingly and with propriety. Sometimes it succeeds too well, so that the audience's attention becomes focused upon the humor as an end in itself rather than as a means of making the message interesting.

A much more thorough treatment of humor will be found in a later chapter when we discuss special speech types. For the present we simply admonish you to label humour "Handle With Care."

SUMMARY

The speaker should strive to get his audience to listen without exerting too much conscious effort. Forced, or voluntary attention, tends to be of short duration, while effortless, or involuntary attention, may be sustained for lengthy periods. The speaker's message may be infused with interest ingredients that elicit the listeners' involuntary attention. Interest may be derived from associating your ideas with something recent, something impending, something physically near, something familiar, something vital, something active, something unusual, something suspenseful, something concrete, something real, something human, something in conflict, and something humorous.

SUGGESTED READINGS

A. CRAIG BAIRD, and FRANKLIN H. KNOWER, *Essentials of General Speech*, (New York: McGraw-Hill Book Company, Inc., 1952). Chapter 17.

DONALD C. BRYANT, and KARL R. WALLACE, *Fundamentals of Public Speaking*, (New York: Appleton-Century-Crofts, Inc., 1947). Chapter 3.

S. Judson Crandall, Gerald M. Phillips, and Joseph A. Wigley, *Speech: A Course in Fundamentals.* (Chicago: Scott, Foresman and Company, 1963). Chapter 10.

J. A. Deutsch, and D. Deutsch, "Attention: Some Theoretical Considerations," *Psychological Review,* 70 (1963), 61-79.

Alan H. Monroe, *Principles and Types of Speech,* 5th edition, (Chicago: Scott, Foresman and Co., 1962). Chapter 13.

Robert T. Oliver, *The Psychology of Persuasive Speech,* (New York: Longmans, Green and Company, 1957). Chapter 6.

Edward Rogge, and James C. Ching, *Advanced Public Speaking,* (New York: Holt, Rinehart and Winston, Inc., 1966). Chapter 2.

Wayne N. Thompson, and Seth A. Fessenden, *Basic Experiences in Speech,* 2nd edition, (Englewood Cliffs, N. J.: Prentice-Hall, Inc., 1958). Chapter 11.

Andrew Thomas Weaver, and Ordean Gerhard Ness, *An Introduction to Public Speaking,* (New York: The Odyssey Press, Inc., 1961). Chapter 9.

Eugene E. White, *Practical Public Speaking,* 2nd edition, (New York: The Macmillan Company, 1964). Chapter 6.

VIII

LANGUAGE

A MEDIUM OF COMMUNICATION

For as long as men have been writing down their thoughts on public speaking and communication they have devoted large sections of their books to the problems of language. This emphasis on the words we use is quite understandable. Our choice of words, as a symbolic code, represents what we mean and feel and what we want others to know. This use of language enables us to "keep in touch" with our fellow human beings. By using language we get people to respond to our thoughts, we change their behavior, and we influence our environment. People gain impressions of us through our language, and are quick to decide what they think of us and our cause by the words we use.

We depend on verbal accounts for our knowledge of almost everything outside the range of our own senses and experiences. We make decisions, run our lives and develop many of our attitudes on the basis of what we hear. Realizing these facts about language and its influence, the student of communication should ask himself two questions: Do my verbal accounts give the listener a true picture of reality? Does my word selection really convey to others the impressions I want to make? The answers to these two questions will serve as the basis for this chapter. First, we will examine those principles and techniques of language usage that will help your material come closer to the life-facts (reality), and second, we will examine those principles and techniques that will enable others to see and feel what you are talking about.

LANGUAGE TO REPRESENT REALITY

LANGUAGE, in the broad sense, is usually defined as a set of symbols used in a common and uniform way by a number of people who are thus able to manipulate these symbols for the purpose of communication. We have already mentioned many of the elements of non-verbal symbols, such as facial expressions, gestures, posture and the like. Now we are primarily concerned with that form of language in which words are the basic symbols. More specifically, in this first section we will discuss those aspects of language that can, depending on their use, either help or hinder an accurate symbolic representation of reality. As you read over these ideas keep in mind that it is through language that we know about the past, live in the present, and prepare for the future.

Words Are Only Symbols

Because words are the basic symbols of verbal language, it is important to remember that they are purely *arbitrary symbols*. We call them symbols because they are used to *represent* objects, ideas, concepts or feelings. The word dog may well stand for a four-legged, domesticated animal, but the *word* "dog" is actually *not* the dog, but rather a sound that our society, and past generations, have decided upon to *stand for* that particular thing. You will also notice that we used the word *arbitrary*—there is no necessary relationship between the word and the thing it stands for. People often forget this fact and confuse a word with the thing for which it stands. They lose sight of the principle that a word exists only as a representation of a fact—a word is not the fact, thing or occurrence to which it refers. Consequently, there is no assurance that the word selected represents or depicts reality. If Senator X calls his opponent "dishonest" and accuses him of "stealing," these symbols may not accurately represent actuality.

The conscientious communicator must always remember that the word is not the thing itself; it is a symbol. He should develop the habit of asking, "Do the words fit the facts?" Irving Lee, in his book *Language Habits in Human Affairs,* summarized this view when he noted that the communicator should not only be concerned with what *it* was called (symbols), but also what *was* being so called (object).

Words Can Have Many Uses

It would indeed be convenient if we had one word for each thing or occurrence. But we are faced with the fact that a limited number of words must serve to cover an unlimited number of things. Wendell Johnson, a writer in the field of general semantics, underscored the problem when he wrote, "A rather large share of our misunderstanding and disagreement arises not so much because we are constitutionally stupid or stubborn, but simply because we have to use the same words to refer to so many different things."

We could cite an endless number of examples for those words that have many uses and meanings. Take the simple word "foot." It can represent a part of the body, a means of measuring, or it can be used as a slang expression. A glance at any standard dictionary will reveal numerous words with twenty-five or more meanings.

Due to this multiple-meaning characteristic of our language we must be very careful when we use symbols that have a variety of meanings. An *awareness* that any word may have a whole list of uses is perhaps the first step in handling the problem. Another step is to realize that what is being said may not represent what the user intended or assumed. In conversation one can also develop the habit of asking directly how a person is using a particular word or phrase. In addition, as speakers, we should try to select words that lend themselves to direct translation and also define those words and phrases that have a variety of meanings.

Words Often Omit Essential Details

Whenever we think or talk about a situation we make decisions as to what to include and what to leave out. We abstract some of the details from the total situation and ignore others. This means, in a very real sense, that when we use language we are only giving a partial picture of what happened. When we say to someone, "Let me tell you about the race riot I saw last night," we are about to make certain selections as to what to talk about and what not to talk about. We can not, by the very nature of our language and our processes of perception, tell our listener each detail we perceived and experienced. We must, therefore, select what we deem important and worth communicating.

Two rather obvious problems present themselves as we make selections. First, what is left out is often more important and vital than what is retained and talked about. Second, our selections of what to talk about are governed by our pre-conceived attitudes and our past experiences—*we* decide what to tell and what not to tell.

It is the awareness of the problems, and the realization that details are omitted, that must be kept uppermost in the minds of both sender and receiver as they engage in communication. Writers in the field of general semantics suggest that as communicators we should learn to wait, to stop and see if more is to be said, and then reach our conclusions; further, that we should develop the use of the ETC., silently or orally, to remind us of the concept that factors are left out. In short, we should remind ourselves that there is always more than can be said.

Word Meanings Are in People

Words, as language symbols, have no meanings in themselves; their real meanings are in the things or events for which they stand. Each person, acting as an individual, must decide what a symbol means to him. Take the word "school." To the person who likes education it is a place of learning, to the boy who hates school it means a place he is made to go, and to still another individual, who desires an education, it means a place where he would like to go. What the word means depends on an individual's experience with the thing or occurrence the word is representing. No two people ever have exactly the same experiences, so consequently no single word has an identical meaning for two people. But the speaker must at least try to select words, phrases and ideas that approach this ideal of common meaning. If understanding, and hence communication, is to take place, the sender and receiver must share a reasonably common code.

LANGUAGE TO INDUCE DESIRED RESPONSES

The language of speechmaking, in addition to being characterized by the four features just discussed, has the auxiliary purpose of making the idea seem real and meaningful. It is not enough to have the idea expressed in everyday language; to have a lasting impression the message must be clear and vivid. The way the speaker selects and uses his words—the proper word in the proper place—is often the first method of distinguishing the most able speakers from all the rest.

A person's style in using words is a highly personal matter, and something which is developed over a long period of time. This does not mean that a person's language habits cannot be improved with practice. On the contrary, the basic elements of effective style and word choice can be amended and enriched by sincere and careful practice. What follows is a listing and discussion of those language elements which can help the speaker accomplish his overall objective, which, in most instances, is to secure a desired response.

Your Language Should Be Clear

As a speaker you must first of all know exactly what idea you wish to convey to your listeners. Then you must find those symbols that will enable you to be understood—to be clear. Clear language is language which is *immediately meaningful* to those who hear it. The speaker who can arouse definite and specific meanings has an excellent chance of being understood. Conversely, the speaker whose language suffers from ambiguity and confusion is not easily comprehended. Clarity can be fostered if the speaker's choice of language is ACCURATE and SIMPLE.

Accurate Language

Being accurate when one speaks involves selecting words which "say what you mean." How often we hear someone say, "I read this book one day," never indicating what book and what day; or he refers to "that thing over there," without ever letting the listener know what "thing" is being talked about. In both cases the language lacks accuracy. Words have been selected which fail to correspond directly with the concept or thing being discussed.

Inaccuracy in word choice is normally brought about by carelessness. The speaker will often use technical language or uncommon words without stopping to realize that the symbols he has selected have very little meaning for his audience. His laziness may also show itself in his failure to seek words which are definite and exact. He may use ambiguous words, which, by their very nature, are not accurate and clear. He may also be guilty of omitting essential details.

Accuracy is enhanced if the speaker selects specific and concrete words. The listener will receive a much clearer picture of what is being talked about if the speaker will use names, dates, places, facts and other details. For example, "On Tuesday John and I went to the Main Street draft board" is certainly more accurate and meaningful than the phrase "I went away with a friend." Or how often we hear statements such as "The United States spent a lot of money on foreign-aid." The communicator who is concerned with clarity and comprehension would say, "In 1962 Congress passed a foreign-aid bill which appropriated 3.6 billion dollars." Here again we see the value of being accurate—the listener knows what we mean.

Simple Language

Short, simple words enhance clarity and understandability. Notice the difference in clarity between "moderate" and "abstemious," "money" and "legal tender," "top" and *ne plus ultra.* Once again it is worth noting that the purpose of communication is to share ideas, information and feelings. If your language distorts the concept you wish to convey, your communication act will fail. By being an exhibitionist with your vocabulary you run the risk of not being understood, and hence, of not accomplishing your purpose.

In closing, it should be remembered that being simple does not mean one is infantile and dull. It indicates that the speaker realizes that words which are vague and complicated can cause serious communication breakdowns.

Your Language Should Be Vivid

Language which is clear will be understood, but if you wish also to hold attention, maintain interest, and create a favorable impression you must make your language vivid as well. This does not mean that vividness and clarity are necessarily separate. On the contrary, in order to achieve vividness you must first of all be clear.

When one talks of being vivid he is normally talking about selecting those words and phrases which are sensory. Vivid language seeks to appeal to the senses of the listener by having him see, hear, feel, taste and smell the images the speaker tries to create.

Imagery

When one is employing imagery he may be asking his listeners to re-encounter a past situation, or to experience a new situation that he paints for them. In either case the main objective is to have the audience experience, vicariously, the particular sensation being described.

1. DETAIL is essential in painting word pictures for the audience. Notice the difference in effectiveness between "A water-skier hit the dock," and "The water-skier, gliding gracefully over the glass-top lake, failed to see the half-sunken dock protruding out into the still water, and went crashing into the exposed wooden beams."

Consider these images:

a. As we drove through the sandy and dusty area we felt the earth beneath us tremble as the wild boars stampeded in front of us.

b. I felt as cold as a piece of ice as I approached the half open door of the broken down cabin.

c. The dazzling brilliance of the setting sun made it difficult for me to see the large figure moving across the stream.

d. His face, touched by time, was rough, scarred and firm.

e. As we entered the room an odor of sweet peppermint lead us to the copper pan sitting on top of the coal-fed stove.

f. As I left the hospital I could still hear the piercing, penetrating cry of the wounded American.

2. Using DESCRIPTIVE ADJECTIVES AND ADVERBS gives the listener a much more complete picture of what is being talked about. "A bitterly cold day," "A studious man," "a damaging admission," and "a sarcastic professor," all offer the listener a more vivid concept of what is being referred to.

3. Images should be selected in light of the listener's BACKGROUND and EXPERIENCES. It is hard for someone to appreciate the "blue and rolling waves that break on the Solomon Islands" if they have never seen the Solomons. Compare the idea to something from the listener's past and the image will be made more effective.

Figures of Speech

Vividness is also achieved by using figures of speech. The figure of speech normally shows itself as a METAPHOR. This device compares objects and concepts which are basically alike. When Abraham Lincoln was talking about the danger of two Americas he used a metaphor: "A house divided against itself cannot stand." A speaker talking about John F. Kennedy's strength used a metaphor when he stated, "Kennedy's heart is as gold, but his convictions are like pillars of marble."

The speaker may also find that his style can be made more vivid by using ANTITHESIS. In this figure of speech contrast is emphasized by the position of words. For example, "The state exists for man, not man for the state." Former President Kennedy used this technique in his now famous phrase, "Ask not what your country can do for you—ask what you can do for your country."

ANALOGIES, which were discussed in detail in Chapter V, are also useful in making ideas and information more vivid.

Language Should Be Appropriate

The words you select to accomplish your purpose should be suited to the occasion and the audience. You will recall that when we discussed the principles of audience analysis (Chapter II) we stressed the importance of knowing all you could about the people you were to address. The educational level of your audience will greatly influence your selection of words and imagery. We have all heard of the speaker who offends his listeners by talking down to them, or the speaker who overestimates the intellectual background of the listener and chooses words that are not fully meaningful to that group. Furthermore, we stressed the importance of knowing all you could about the occasion. A small gathering of close personal friends would call for less formal language than a commencement address. A careful analysis of the audience and occasion will enable you to adjust your language to fit the occupational level, intelligence level, background, attitudes and interests of your listeners.

Language Should Be Free from Distractions

All of us tend to have some poor language habits which interfere with our overall effectiveness in communicating. We inadvertently select words and phrases that distract from our main ideas and thereby "de-rail" our message.

SLANG

Slang words and phrases are sometimes acceptable, but more often they tend to lower the status of the user. The person who must resort to slang is following the line of least resistance; it takes effort to find the right word. Phrases such as "guys," "cool," "sharp," "real great," and "behind the eight ball," do little to clarify an idea, make an image vivid, or raise the speaker's credibility.

TRITENESS

Closely related to slang is the problem of trite and hackneyed phrases. Speakers who are reduced to employing overworked expressions such as "pretty as a picture," "last but not least," "our hour of trial," and "it gives me great pleasure," clearly reveal their lack of imagination and education.

JARGON

When a speaker is addressing a general audience he must avoid shoptalk, jargon and highly technical language. Each profession has its own language, and the speaker must remember that what is clear to an engineer may be very confusing to the doctor. If the symbols selected are not easily defined, ambiguity will result. "Cognitive dissonance-consonance" may be quite meaningful to the social psychologist, but it is only noise to the layman. Knowing your listener's background and defining unfamiliar words will help you overcome many of the problems of jargon.

"BIG" WORDS

There are many speakers who would rather exhibit their vocabulary than be understood. These individuals will avoid the short, hard-hitting, accurate word for the long and supposedly impressive one. They will say "edifice" instead of "building," "surreptitiously" instead of "secret," and "imbibe" instead of "drink." Admittedly, there will be occasions when the "big" word is appropriate, but good style calls for the best word at the best place.

LOADED WORDS

There are those who would suggest that loaded and emotional words should be used whenever possible. They would argue that such words assist the speaker in his goal of "manipulating others." Although loaded words are often colorful they are in most instances ambiguous and vague. By playing upon emotionalism these words, both implicitly and explicitly, ask the listener to respond on a purely emotional basis. Notice the images which are called forth by phrases such as "the savage and brutal senator," "the chiseling miser," "the bureaucratic welfare state," and "a fanatical right-winger." Granting that emotion is important in communication, the speaker should supply adequate evidence and sound reasoning to justify any loaded word he uses. He should remember that the words he uses must be consistent with the real facts. If a colorful word can be selected that doesn't distort reality it should be used, but if the appeal is solely an irrational one the speaker is then violating his ethical responsibility.

EMPTY WORDS

In this day of the mass appeal we are constantly being exposed to superlatives and exaggerations. This over-exposure may well condition the unsuspecting communicator to lean heavily on the overworked and meaningless term. Notice the empty quality of the following words and phrases: "super," "colossal," "deluxe," "terrific," "very good," "fantastic," "extra special," and "a whole lot." We are members of an age where many people have been so bombarded with empty words that they are tempted to discount them and pay little attention to the person who uses them.

IMPROVING OUR LANGUAGE

Language habits and vocabulary develop early in life, and cannot be quickly improved by memorizing some simple laws or formulas. Yet there are a few practices that can help the student alter, adjust and improve his use of language.

1. *Learn to use a dictionary and book of synonyms.* These two sources are helpful in that they provide the student with clues to new words which are often more accurate and vivid than the ones he has been using.

2. *Learn to listen for new words.* This is an excellent way to enrich one's vocabulary while increasing your knowledge of a subject being discussed.

3. *Look for new words in your reading.* This includes the reading of novels, plays, speeches and essays. All of these offer examples of how very talented people use language.

4. *Develop a habit of careful writing.* Careful writing and revision tends to develop better expression. If the writer is diligent, he will not jot down the first word that comes to his mind, but will search for the word or phrase that will promote clarity and convey the desired impression.

5. *Speaking often* is one of the obvious ways of learning to use language well. By actually "doing the thing," the speaker learns which words and phrases help him in accomplishing his purpose and which words will retard his efforts.

6. *Be aware of words and make a study of language itself.* The field of General Semantics, for example, seeks to examine

the relationship between language and things. The sincere student will find this sort of study both rewarding and interesting. There is a whole new world to explore when one investigates how people use symbols to influence one another and the world they live in.

Most of the elements discussed in this book apply to improving one's ability to use words. For example, language should be interesting to listen to and easy to comprehend. Both of these concepts are discussed in detail in other sections of this book, attention and interest in Chapter V, informing in Chapter X. At the conclusion of Chapter VII we examined some common language fallacies and how to avoid them. We can therefore conclude by noting that the study of speech is in part a study of language improvement.

SUMMARY

Keep these general language principles in mind as you engage in both public and private communication: (1) Words are only symbols that are used to represent objects, ideas, concepts or feelings. (2) One word can have many meanings and many uses. (3) In using symbols as our communication code we often omit essential details. (4) Word meanings reside within people; they have meaning only in terms of the associations established between the symbols and the objects or concepts to which they refer.

Clarity, vividness and appropriateness characterize effective language usage. Clarity derives from the use of words that are accurate, simple, and precise. Vividness derives from imagery, which is accomplished by use of details and descriptive words, and from figures of speech. Appropriateness derives from using language that is suited to the audience, occasion, and speaker, and avoiding slang, triteness, jargon, "big" words, loaded words, and empty words. One's language can be improved by sincere and conscientious study and practice.

SUGGESTED READINGS

JOHN W. BLACK, and WILBUR E. MOORE, Speech: Code, Meaning, and Communication, (New York: McGraw-Hill Book Company, Inc., 1955). Chapter 10.

MAX BLACK, ed., The Importance of Language, (Englewood Cliffs, N. J.: Prentice-Hall, Inc., 1962).

GLADYS BORCHERS, "An Approach to the Problem of Oral Style," Quarterly Journal of Speech, 22 (1936), 114-117.

RUDOLF FLESCH, The Art of Plain Talk, (New York: Harper and Brothers, 1946).

H. I. HAYAKAWA, Language in Thought and Action, (New York: Harcourt, Brace and World, 1949).

IRVING J. LEE, How to Talk with People, (New York: Harper and Row, 1962).

IRVING J. LEE, Language Habits in Human Affairs, (New York: Harper and Brothers, 1941).

WENDELL JOHNSON, People in Quandaries, (New York: Harper and Row, 1946).

SUZANNE K. LANGER, Philosophy in a New Key, (Cambridge: Harvard University Press, 1942).

GLENN E. MILLS, Composing the Speech, (Englewood Cliffs, N. J.: Prentice-Hall, 1952). Chapter 14.

STEPHEN ULLMANN, Language and Style, (New York: Barnes and Noble, Inc., 1964).

IX

PERSUASIVE COMMUNICATION

CHANGING BEHAVIOR

The teenager trying to talk his father out of the family car for the evening, the public relations man explaining to a civic club how his utility company enables modern man to enjoy a more leisurely life, the historian attempting to prove to a scholarly convention that a certain "fact" of history is really a myth, all are engaged in what we call PERSUASIVE COMMUNICATION. The immediate aim of the teenager is to induce action; the immediate aim of the public relations man is to create (or reinforce) a favorable attitude toward his firm, and the immediate aim of the historian is to win agreement from his colleagues. In a real sense, of course, the *ultimate* aim of all three is to induce action. Continued patronage of his company is the ultimate aim of the public relations man, and the incorporation into historical scholarship of his finding is the ultimate aim of the historian.

Persuasion, then, MAY BE DEFINED AS THE ART OF INDUCING OTHERS TO BELIEVE, TO FEEL, OR TO ACT IN A WAY THAT IS PREDETERMINED BY THE SPEAKER. Speeches whose immediate aim is to induce belief are sometimes called speeches to CONVINCE.

Those aiming at reinforcing existing beliefs, attitudes, and emotions are called speeches to STIMULATE. And those aiming at inducing action are called speeches to ACTUATE. For our purposes, we shall simply call them speeches to persuade.

THE AUDIENCE AND PERSUASION

We have repeatedly called attention to the importance of audience analysis in this text. If the aim of persuasion is to induce a behavioral change in the listener, then it behooves us to place particular emphasis upon knowing the listener. It is probable that the majority of failures in persuasive attempts can be traced to insufficient or inaccurate analysis of those the speaker wishes to influence. Perhaps the speaker has taken pains to find out about his listeners as individuals but has failed to take into account what they are like when they become members of a group. The group imposes codes of behavior upon the individual that are not necessarily operative when he is removed from the group. The salesman who is accustomed to dealing with one person at a time sometimes finds it a difficult experience to deal with a crowd, so different are people in their public and private behavior. On the other hand, there are those who find it easier to deal with the crowd than with the individual, because of the tendency of most people to become less critical in their thinking when they become members of a crowd. At any rate, the speaker should become familiar with what *motivates* the listener as an individual and as a member of a group.

The following are some of the possible individual and group attitudes that will confront the speaker at the outset of a persuasive speech. (1) Individual listeners or the audience as a whole may be apathetic toward your proposition. If that be the case, you may have to place particular stress upon the link between your proposition and the listeners' self-interests in order to overcome the apathy. (2) Individual listeners or the audience as a whole may be hostile toward the point of view you are espousing. This may involve your starting with those items with which you and the audience are in agreement, and then moving on to the areas of disagreement. (3) Individual listeners or the audience as a whole may be interested but undecided, in which case you may decide to place particular emphasis upon the use of factual evidence which supports your position. (4) Individual listeners or the audience as a whole may be favorably inclined toward your position. Your job, in that case, is to reaffirm for the listeners their bases for agreeing with you. (5) Individual listeners or the audience as a whole may be primarily concerned with your personal credibility. If you have a good reputation preceding you to the platform, then your task is to confirm that reputation. If you have a negative reputation before the speech, your job is to supplant it with a positive reputation. And if you have no reputation preceding you to the platform, then your job is to create a good one through the speech itself.

THE COMMON TOPICS OF PERSUASION

When we attempt to induce belief, feeling, and action, we are usually dealing with (1) propositions involving the advisability of a proposed POLICY; (2) propositions concerning the actuality of an alleged FACT; and (3) propositions concerning the validity of a VALUE judgment. In the first instance the speaker is concerned with such issues as whether or not a problem exists, whether or not it is a serious problem, whether or not the proposed solution will correct the problem, whether or not the proposed solution is the best one of all those available. These are the issues that arise whenever men debate questions of POLICY, such as whether the U. S. should continue to support the Alliance for Progress program in Latin America. In the case of propositions of FACT, the speaker is maintaining that something is or is not so—that we are winning the war against poverty, that inflation will result if a wage hike is granted, that the defendant did not commit the crime. In the case of propositions of VALUE, the speaker is maintaining that something is good or bad, is better than something else, is worthy or unworthy, is justified or unjustified. For example, he might maintain that

James Baldwin is the most eloquent spokesman of the negro cause. These three general areas then, represent the common topics of persuasion. It should be noted that issues of fact, value, and policy may all arise during the course of a single speech. For example, a speaker trying to win support for a proposed policy probably will have to prove that there is a need for the policy (proposition of fact), that his policy will fulfill the need (proposition of fact) and that his policy is better than any other policy that might be proposed (proposition of value).

The precise issues with which you should deal in a given communication situation will depend upon the audience. Through careful analysis of the audience you should determine *where they are in their thinking about the subject.* If your speech involves a QUESTION OF POLICY, you should ask:

1. Does the audience know that a problem exists?
2. Are they aware of the extent of the problem?
3. Are they aware of the causes of the problem?
4. Are they aware of the various possible solutions to the problem?
5. Are they aware of the advantages and disadvantages of some or all of the solutions?
6. Are they favorably disposed toward a particular solution?
7. How do they feel toward my solution?

If you discover that the audience is unaware of the existence of a problem, then you may well spend one entire speech in establishing that fact to their satisfaction. Or perhaps you discover that their thinking has evolved to the stage of considering and weighing the various solutions. In that case, you may devote your speech solely to showing the superior merits of your solution. It is possible, of course, that you may, in a single speech, deal with all of the issues suggested above.

If your speech is limited to a QUESTION OF FACT OR A QUESTION OF VALUE, then you need to ask:

1. By what criteria would my audience measure the "truth" of the alleged fact or the validity of the value judgement?
2. Are the criteria the audience would use really valid?
3. Are there better criteria?

For example, in a criminal case guilt may be measured by motive, means, and opportunity. The contending attorneys apply these criteria to the evidence at hand. A salesman who wants to convince a customer that his product is superior to a competitor's product should know the customer's criteria for what constitutes superiority. Is the superior product the one that is the most efficient, the most attractive, the most prestigious to own, the most economical, the safest, the cleanest? Unless the salesman discovers the criteria (and the priority of criteria) used by the customer he isn't likely to consummate the sale. This does not mean that he will necessarily *use* the customer's criteria. He may try to convince the customer that there are other criteria that are even more important.

THE MODES OF PERSUASION

Twenty-four centuries ago Aristotle in his *Rhetoric* observed that there are three instruments of persuasion: (1) ". . . persuasion is effected by the ARGUMENTS, when we demonstrate the truth, real or apparent, by such means as inhere in particular cases." (2) ". . . persuasion is effected through the audience, when they are brought by the speech into a state of EMOTION; for we give very different decisions under the sway of pain or joy, and liking or hatred." (3) "The CHARACTER of the speaker is a cause of persuasion when the speech is so uttered as to make him worthy of belief; for as a rule we trust men of probity more, and more quickly, about things in general, while on points outside the realm of exact knowledge, where opinion is divided, we trust them absolutely." The durability of Aristotle's classification may be seen by a cursory examination of rhetorical treatises from his day to the present. Perhaps different labels are affixed to the modes of persuasion, and perhaps some of the modes have been subdivided, but all are essentially Aristotelean in their origin. In this chapter we shall use, in addition to the three traditional Aristotelean modes, a fourth mode. Thus we shall discuss: (1) persuasion through LOGICAL APPEALS, (2) persuasion through INFORMATION,

(3) persuasion through PSYCHOLOGICAL APPEALS, and (4) persuasion through the speaker's PERSONAL CREDIBILITY.

It should be emphasized that this separation of persuasion into four modes is purely arbitrary. In most communication situations the speaker's persuasive attempts will be a composite of all of these modes. In short, we suggest you view these four as being fused together in practice, even though we are analyzing them separately.

Persuasion Through Logical Appeals

Rational grounds for belief or action are generally regarded as the most durable and desirable of all. We like to think that any action we take or any belief or attitude we cherish rests upon a solid foundation of reason. Aristotle thought that reason should be the sole determinant of actions, but he recognized human frailty and grudgingly acknowledged that reason often had to be accompanied by non-rational (but not irrational) determinants. As we indicated, our position shall be that all four modes of persuasion are likely to be operative in a speech, some used more extensively than others, depending upon the dictates of the particular communication situation. As we discuss persuasion through logic, then, bear in mind that it will, in all likelihood, be accompanied by the other modes of persuasion.

The vital constituents of the logical mode of persuasion are evidence and reasoning.

EVIDENCE

A thorough analysis of evidence (forms of support) was undertaken in Chapter V. It would be well for you to review that material as part of your introduction to persuasive communication. What follows, therefore, is a description of how various forms of evidence can be applied specifically to persuasive speaking. We shall group the forms of evidence into the following two general categories: (1) evidence of FACT, and (2) evidence of OPINION.

FACTUAL EVIDENCE may be drawn from the speaker's own personal observation or from external sources. Each of us has witnessed some event and then reported to others what we have witnessed. Perhaps we were on the scene of an automobile accident, and we tell the investigating officer the details of what happened. Or we argue with a friend over which super-market has the lowest prices, and we cite to him the actual prices we have paid for a particular grocery item. The valid-ity of factual evidence drawn from our own personal observa-tion is dependent upon two factors. First, how well equipped are we to be good witnesses of the "facts" we report? Do we have the necessary physical capacities, such as keen eyesight, or acute hearing? Is our perception colored by the emotional state we happen to be in? Do we see only what we want to see? In short, are we objective observers? Second, how well equipped are we to report what we have seen? Do we alter the story from telling to telling to make it more interesting? Do we relish the lurid details out of proportion to their im-portance? Do we possess the kind of vocabulary needed for relatively objective reporting.

Factual evidence drawn from external sources must meet these and other tests of validity. Is the fact being reported directly by the original observer? If so, that observer should be judged in light of the same questions we ask ourselves when we are the primary observers. Is the fact being reported by a secondary source? If so, what is the secondary source's repu-tation for reliability? When was the fact observed and when was it reported? What is fact today may not be fact tomor-row (witness population figures!). Is the fact represented out of context? Do other sources report the same fact?

OPINION EVIDENCE also has two sources—the speaker's own personal opinions based upon his experience and the opinions of others, presumably experts. The acceptability of the speaker's "educated guess" is, of course, dependent upon whether the audience views him as a person qualified to voice an informed opinion. If by reason of your occupation or your major field of study you do possess the necessary qualifications for expert-ness—and if your audience recognizes these qualifications as adequate—then you may with impunity use yourself as a source of opinion. By and large, however, the student speaker will utilize the testimony of a recognized authority. Whether the opinion cited is his own or an expert's it should meet the criteria for valid testimony discussed in Chapter V.

REASONING.

The mere possession of valid evidence of fact and opinion is, of course, valueless unless we do something with it. The process of "doing something with" evidence—that is, drawing conclusions from it—is called REASONING. As you have doubtless seen, the same set of facts and opinions can lead to more than one conclusion. The persuasive speaker attempts to show that his conclusions are nearer to "truth" than those of his opponent.

We generally recognize four forms of reasoning: (1) deduction, (2) induction, (3) reasoning from analogy, and (4) reasoning from causation.

1. DEDUCTIVE REASONING. This is also called reasoning from axiom and reasoning from the general to the particular. The familiar syllogism,

> All men are mortals.
> Socrates is a man.
> Therefore, Socrates is a mortal.

is often cited as an example of deductive reasoning. The first line, "All men are mortals," is the axiom, or general statement. The second line is the particular case in point, "Socrates is a man." The third line states the conclusion, which shows the relationship of the particular to the general. Much of our reasoning follows this pattern. We have countless axioms which we employ in making everyday decisions. We have axioms to guide us in selecting a movie to see—"Movies starring Tamara Beachead are interesting movies. I see one is playing at the Lyric. Let's go!" Others guide us in where to eat out—"The tacos at Nina's are fabulous. I'm hungry for a taco. Let's go to Nina's." Others guide in picking professors—"The Faculty Register is a reliable guide. I'm going to follow its advice and crash Professor Tower's class." Needless to say, our reasoning is not 100% foolproof!

Several tests should be applied as a means of detecting potential weak spots in our use of the deductive method. First of all, is the axiom or general rule usually true? Are Tamara Beachead's movies usually interesting? Why do you say so? How many of her movies have you seen? Is your axiom based on personal experience or on the judgment of a friend or perhaps a professional movie critic? Unless the axiom is usually true, then the conclusion will not be usually true. (You will note that we use the word *usually*. The persuasive speaker deals in the main with what is probable rather than what is certain.) Secondly, does the particular case in point fall within the scope of the axiom? Does the movie playing at the Lyric really *star* Tamara Beachead, or does she simply play a cameo role? Is it a feature she made ten years ago before she was regarded as a star? Unless the case in point falls within the scope of the axiom we cannot validly conclude that the movie at the Lyric will probably be interesting.

Persuasive speaking is replete with use of deductive reasoning. When we urge others to defeat welfare legislation "because it's socialistic," we are saying in essence:

> Socialism is bad.
> Welfare legislation is socialistic.
> Therefore, it is bad. (And we don't support bad things.)

It behooves us as speakers and as listeners to examine critically any use of deductive reasoning. Unless the deduction can meet the tests mentioned above, it is spurious.

2. INDUCTION. Also called reasoning from examples, reasoning from the specific to the general, or simply generalization, induction is the reverse of deduction. The pollster interviews 500 voters and concludes that "The American voter is more conservative than he was ten years ago." We read that four locals of the International Speech Fabricators are rife with corruption and conclude that all the other locals are probably corrupt, or possibly that all labor unions are corrupt. We meet a beautiful exchange student from Ceylon and then tell our friends that

Ceylon has the most beautiful girls in the world. All of these examples are imperfect inductions in that the generalization is based upon a limited number of examples. However, it is usually impossible for us to investigate every single part of the whole; so, we must rely upon what we feel is a representative sampling. The professional pollster has perfected the means of obtaining a representative sampling to the extent that his services command high respect (and high prices).

All of us engage in inductive reasoning. In fact, many of the axioms we employ in deductive reasoning have been arrived at through a prior process of induction. The axiom, "Movies starring Tamara Beachead are interesting movies," was probably arrived at after the viewer had witnessed three or four of her movies.

Since we all use induction we should be familiar with the tests of its validity. The following questions are pertinent. (1) How many examples are used in arriving at the generalization? To sample two watermelons from an entire truckload and then generalize about the whole truckload is to trust to luck rather than to logical reasoning. There must be *enough* examples to warrant the conclusion drawn. (2) How representative of the whole class are the examples which are used in generalizing about the class? While the *quantity* of examples is important, even more important is the *quality* of the examples. Permitted by the indulgent storekeeper to sample three apples from a bushel basket, could you choose a representative sampling of the entire basket? Perhaps not because of the limited quantity. But at least you could make an intelligent attempt. Would you choose your three apples from the top? From the middle layer? From the bottom layer? Very likely you would choose one from each layer. Or if the storekeeper has a reputation for packing fruit of uniform quality, then conceivably one apple from the basket might warrant a generalization about the whole. (3) Is the generalization confined to the class from which the examples were drawn? Alluding to our apple-sampling example, any generalization we draw should be concerned only with the basket from which the sampling was made, not with all the baskets in

the store. Yet this is a common error in induction. One rene-
gade labor union gives a black eye to all organized labor. The
misbehavior of a few teenagers in Chicago is used as the basis
for a generalization about all teenagers, when at best it should
be used as a basis for generalizing about certain Chicago young-
sters. As a listener you should apply these tests of inductive
logic to the remarks of the speaker. As a speaker you should
make certain that your inductive reasoning meets these tests
before employing it.

3. REASONING FROM ANALOGY. "It will never work here. It
didn't work in Sweden." "Try my headache remedy. It'll make
you feel better in a hurry." "I don't see why I can't have a new
car. George's dad bought him one." In each of the examples
cited, the speaker is drawing upon comparisons to reach his
conclusion. In the first example there is an implied comparison
between Sweden and "here." In the second, there is a comparison between "you and me" or my headache and yours. And in
the final example, George and "I" or George's dad and my
dad are things compared. Reasoning from analogy, then, suggests that because two things are alike in certain known respects they will also be alike with respect to the issue in question.
Of all the forms of reasoning, this is perhaps the one most subject to error—and for a very simple reason. The validity of any
argument based upon comparison is contingent upon a high degree of similarity existing between the circumstances compared.
A perfect analogy would demand identical circumstances with
no variables involved. Such circumstances are seldom ever
found to exist. Thus the person using analogical reasoning must
be extremely careful to avoid overlooking pertinent point of
dissimilarity between two otherwise comparable things.

What are the *relevant* points of similarity that should exist
in the items compared? The physician is trained to recognize
relevant points of similarity between the patient at hand and
a patient already treated. Thus he can reason that "Joe has the
same symptoms as Harry. Penicillin treatment worked for Harry;
so I'll prescribe it for Joe." But speakers all too often do not
take the time to analyze the constituents of relevancy. Noting

that a great *number* of similarities exist between two situations, they don't take the time to ask if the similarities are pertinent. Don't be fooled by quantity; look for quality.

If you expect to employ reasoning from analogy in a speech, it would be advisable to utilize one or more of the other forms of reasoning as well because of their higher probative value. If you rely solely upon the analogy, your audience may note points of dissimilarity that you have overlooked. Thus all your eggs are broken because of the weak basket.

4. REASONING FROM CAUSAL RELATIONSHIPS. Causation may appear in at least three forms. We may reason from a known set of circumstances to a probable set of consequences, i.e. from cause-to-effect. Conversely, we may reason from a known set of consequences back to their probable cause, effect-to-cause. Or we may reason from one set of consequences to another set of consequences, i.e., from effect-to-effect.

CAUSE-TO-EFFECT reasoning can be readily illustrated. We read in the newspaper that the auto workers have been granted a wage hike, so we predict that the prices on new-model cars will be higher. Or in election years we hear Democrats saying, "Don't elect the Republicans unless you want to get back in the breadline." The Republicans, in turn, say, "Don't elect the Democrats unless you want to get us in another war."

EFFECT-TO-CAUSE reasoning is just as common. The accident scene reeks of alcohol, so we reason that the accident was the result of drunken driving. The next-door neighbor sports a beet-red complexion, so we reason that he stayed too long at the beach. The stock market moves sharply upward, so we conclude it is the result of the President's latest observation on the state of the nation's economy.

EFFECT-TO-EFFECT reasoning is actually a special form of reasoning from analogy. It says that because two sets of circumstances are similar (similar "causes") their consequences will be similar. The doctor who prescribed penicillin for Joe because it worked for Harry, who exhibited the same symptoms, was using both analogical and causal reasoning.

Reasoning from causation should be subjected to the following tests. (1) Does the alleged cause always produce the same effect? (2) Can the effect result from more than one cause? (3) Are there any conditions that can interfere with a causal connection? The typical plot of a television courtroom drama offers some of the examples of debate over causation. The prosecutor contends that the defendant murdered his rich uncle because he had a motive, he had a weapon, and he had an opportunity. These causes produced the known effect—the dead uncle. The defense attorney agrees that the defendant did, indeed, have a motive, a weapon, and an opportunity. But he contends that the defendant did not have the physical capability to bludgeon a man much larger and stronger than he. Then he uncovers evidence that the old reliable family retainer, Harwood, had a motive, a weapon, an opportunity, *and* the physical capability. Thus he was the real cause.

Persuasion Through Information

While his wife is busy trying on dresses in the ladies ready-to-wear department, the parcel-laden husband wanders idly through the housewares section of the large department store. His curiosity is captured by a middle-aged man in a white smock who seems to be cutting, slicing, dicing, and grating miscellaneous chunks of cabbage, carrot, potato, and beet while a small cluster of men, women, and children look on. The white-smocked man says little; he occasionally answers a question. His attention is focused on his work. Our hero steps forward. "How much does one of those gadgets cost?" "Two-ninety-eight." "I'll take one."

Would you say our friend was persuaded to buy the gadget? Not a single syllogism came from the lips of the white-smocked man. He didn't seem to be actively selling. Yet this scene represents one of the most common means of persuasion—the soft-sell approach of persuasion through information or demonstration. The customer seems to be selling himself on the product; yet the most careful planning has gone into the demonstration. It is calculated to arouse curiosity, to make the customer feel a need for the product, to show him how he can fulfill this need by ownership of the product. The crisp, carefully selected vegetables, the honey-colored chopping block, the warm tones of the salad dishes, the precise and skillful movements of the demonstrator are all operating as means of persuasion as surely as would logically-constructed arguments.

You drive your car into a service station. While the automatic pump is filling your gas tank, the attendant checks your oil. "You're almost two quarts low," he says in a matter-of-fact manner. "Well, fill it up with the 10-30 premium grade," you respond. Your action has been triggered by information. The attendant doesn't have to say, "You're almost two quarts low. Therefore, you'd better let me fill it up." He simply provides the information; you draw the inference. In a sense, persuasion through information is but a special form of persuasion through logical appeals. The principal difference is to be found in the fact that in the latter the speaker draws the inference for the listener while in the former the listener draws the inference for himself. Both modes employ evidence; one uses reasoning overtly, the other suggests it.

Persuasion Through Psychological Appeals

A speaker may, with faultless reasoning and unimpeachable evidence, cause you to agree with him that a problem exists and that he has the ideal solution to the problem. Yet you may fail to take the steps necessary to implement his solution. You have been convinced, but you haven't been actuated. Why? The answer may lie in the fact that he talked in terms of "a problem," rather than *your* problem, and that he has offered a solution to "a problem" rather than a solution to *your* problem. In short, he has overlooked the psychologically impelling reasons that spur people to action. Unless the listener can feel some identification with the problem he isn't likely to take action to solve the problem, however logical a given solution might be.

How does the speaker get the listener to IDENTIFY with the problem and the solution? There are two general means. First, if the problem and its solution have a direct bearing upon the life and welfare of the listener, the speaker simply has to point this out. Second, if the problem and its solution affects the listener only indirectly, then the speaker must point out how someone close to the listener is affected (or possibly how someone *who can be made to seem close* to the listener is affected). Perhaps an illustration will clarify these avenues of identification. If you are making a plea for contributions to the cancer fund, and your listeners are themselves cancer victims, then your approach will probably be to point out that augmentation of the cancer fund may mean direct assistance to the listeners. If the audience is made up of those who have relatives or friends who are sufferers, then you will probably stress the warmth of helping out a loved one. If the audience is made up of those who have no connection with anyone who is afflicted, then you may, through a vivid narrative, introduce them to a "typical" cancer victim through whom they can identify with the problem and its solution. Whether the listener feels the problem directly or vicariously HE MUST BE MADE TO FEEL IT IF ACTION IS TO BE FORTHCOMING.

An examination of some of the basic needs, wants, and desires that lie behind human actions may suggest ways in which you can get the audience to identify with your persuasive messages.

1. SELF-PRESERVATION. The person who uses the seat belts that come installed in his new car is typical of those who are motivated to act out of a desire for self-preservation. Safety devices, physical fitness courses, life-prolonging medications are examples of goods and services that provide a partial answer to man's need to stay alive and enjoy physical well-being. Pleas to step up draft quotas or increase military appropriations are usually rooted in one's desire to preserve the nation and hence oneself. For example, a speaker trying to solicit support for an increase in our defense budget might use self-preservation as the appeal by noting, "With the enemy's missiles pointed at our East Coast each of us runs the real risk of becoming a victim of a nuclear warhead unless we take steps immediately to insure a strong anti-missile defense.

2. SEX ATTRACTION. A cursory glance at any magazine, newspaper, billboard or television advertisement will confirm the

power of sex attraction as a motive impelling us to buy an astonishingly wide range of goods and services. Purchase of that new car suggests a bevy of glamorous companions. The new electric typewriter conjures up fantasies of a happy, and hence glamorous, secretary. The public speaker, however, is well-advised to employ this motive more discreetly than the advertiser. People in a group would probably be made to feel uncomfortable by an overt appeal to the sex motive while the same appeal appearing in print would not cause a raised eyebrow. The difference probably lies in our reluctance to acknowledge publicly our susceptibility to this appeal. Therefore, it is preferable to plant a suggestion rather than to openly link your argument with sex attraction.

3. ACQUISITION OF PROPERTY. The appeal to the pocketbook is as popular as the appeal to sex attraction in advertising. Bargain sales, "giant, economy sizes," higher interest rates on savings accounts, real estate speculation are all manifestations of the universal desire among men to acquire property. The spokesman for the school bond drive points out that a better educated citizenry will be a more prosperous citizenry, suggesting that money spent now will be returned many times over as a result of a healthier economy. Even the Rolls Royce ads have occasionally appealed to our desire to save money—in the long run.

4. SELF-ESTEEM. Sometimes we will sacrifice personal safety, eschew sex attraction, and spurn the acquisition of property if it means that our self-esteem can be increased. The desire to be "looked-up-to," to be well-regarded by one's peers, or one's superiors, is a powerful motivating force. It may be manifested in such diverse actions as enrolling in night school, swimming the English channel, donating a large sum to charity, or indulging in conspicious consumption. Self-esteem, extended to groups, takes the form of civic pride, the desire to be "first in the nation," to be the alfalfa-baling center of the country, to have the world's finest zoo.

5. PERSONAL ENJOYMENT. Our love of good food and drink, of comfortable accommodations, of labor-saving devices, of all the so-called "good things in life" becomes a dominant motive once our basic needs for food, clothing, and shelter have been

satisfied. We don't buy sugar for its life-sustaining qualities but for its power to bring pleasure to our taste buds. We don't buy a fifty-thousand dollar home just to keep out the elements but to satisfy our love of the "nicer things." Trailers, campers, power boats, works of art, and stereo phonographs are acquired primarily to satisfy our need for personal enjoyment.

6. CONSTRUCTIVENESS. The week-end mason erecting a con-crete-block retaining wall, the housewife making dresses for her daughters, the retired captain fashioning a brigantine from tooth-picks, cloth, and paste-board are manifesting man's desire to be constructive, creative, inventive. The speaker enlists support for a community clean-up campaign by appealing to the civic club's collective desire for constructive effort.

7. DESTRUCTIVENESS. Man also is motivated by an urge to destroy that which he feels is detrimental to himself, his family, his society. So he is urged to "stamp out crime," conquer disease, rid the nation of poverty, break down the barriers of race, creed, and color, and fight ignorance. In short, he is asked to put his destructive instincts to constructive effort.

8. CURIOSITY. Many things we undertake not simply to gain some tangible benefit therefrom, but rather to satisfy our sense of curiosity. We flock to the balloon-launching, patronize the freak show, buy the paperback book with the enticing cover, or try a "new taste sensation" because we find the unusual and the novel so enticing.

9. IMITATION. The desire to "be just like" some person we admire prompts us to buy the breakfast food recommended by the leading ground gainer in the American Football League, to acquire the same set of encyclopedias owned by our wealthy neighbors, to vote for the political candidate recommended by our favorite movie actor. The speaker must be cautious, however, in appealing to our imitative instincts. He must take pains to discover whether or not the model he wishes us to imitate is really admired by us. If he is envied by us, we may go to great lengths to avoid imitating him.

10. ALTRUISM. We like to think that some of our actions are not selfishly motivated. We make anonymous donations to charity, we send CARE packages abroad, we volunteer to read to the blind, we sacrifice for our country.

The speaker will do well to utilize as many appropriate appeals as possible, for not all members of an audience will be motivated by the same appeal. The hierarchy of needs, wants, and desires is different for each individual. Furthermore, most of us are occasionally impelled by motives we'd rather not admit; so we appreciate the speaker who gives us a "legitimate" motive for doing what we already want to do. Our propensity to rationalize has long been recognized by persuaders on and off the platform.

Even though we have discussed the preceding ten motive appeals as though they were separate entities, they are, in reality, seldom as simple or fixed as we have, for pedagogical purposes, suggested. For, in essence, man is a complicated creature and not subject to simple stimulus-response relationships.

Most human behavior is motivated not by a single act, but rather by a large complex of behavior patterns. For example, most of our actions are related to our past experiences, our emotional tendencies of fighting, fleeing, and pairing, our biological needs, our psychological needs (such as security, recognition, affection, and new experiences), our personal goals and beliefs, and, most of all, our self-concept. It should be obvious, therefore, to the trained speaker that he should not view his receiver as a simple responding organism, but rather as a highly intricate individual.

Suggestion

We are all familiar with the chain reaction set off by the first person in a group to yawn. We recall the delight of "conning" our elders into looking upward at a tall building. We have experienced the magnetic pull toward the carnival barker as we see a small crowd gathering. And the sight of a child carrying a box of popcorn stirs our yearning for the same thing. The power of SUGGESTION is operative in all of these cases.

SUGGESTION may be defined as the arousal of a response by indirect means. It may operate through channels that are external to the message, such as the decor of the surroundings, flags, paintings, posters, giant photographs, acts of ritual, music, and prominently displayed collection plates or cannisters. These factors may operate to condition the listener to respond positively to the speaker's message.

Suggestion operates as well through the speaker's appearance, the sound of his voice, his whole manner on the platform. If he appears to be confident (but not cocky), he tends to stir confidence in what he has to say. If he *seems* to lack assurance (whether he *actually does* is beside the point), the listener tends to be wary of his message. If his posture is slouchy, his ideas, by association, may seem superficial or his thinking sloppy.

Suggestion operates through the speaker's message. If he stresses positive ideas, if he avoids mentioning ideas contrary to his thesis, if he keeps "personalities" out of controversy, he conditions the audience to respond favorably to his point of view (or at least he conditions them against a negative response).

Further ramifications of the influence of suggestion will be apparent in our discussion of the fourth mode of persuasion.

Persuasion Through Personal Credibility

"What you are stands over you the while, and thunders so that I cannot hear what you say to the contrary." Emerson's familiar statement epitomizes the impact of the speaker's ETHOS upon the listener's reception of the message. The way the audience perceives the speaker, as well as the way it perceives his message, determines the nature of its response.

Why do you take your automobile to a certain mechanic for repairs? If you know something of the intricacies of an automobile engine, then your selection of a mechanic may rest on logical grounds. If you are mechanically naive, you may have chosen the mechanic simply because *something about him* inspired confidence.

Speakers on two separate occasions attempt to convince you that a right-to-work law in your state should be repealed. Both use essentially the same arguments and the same evidence. But you want to agree with one of the speakers, while the other speaker cannot manage to budge your convictions. What is the difference? *Something about* the one speaker inspired believability.

What are the constituents of personal credibility? What are the clues we as listeners subconsciously look for in speakers? The following list, while by no means exhaustive, does suggest some facets of speaker behavior to which audiences respond favorably.

1. *Intelligence.* The extent to which a speaker seems to have mastery of his subject matter is a determinant of our response to him. If he marshalls an impressive amount of evidence, if he shows insight into all aspects of the question, if he uses reasoning that meets the tests of logical validity, if he displays "common sense," his believability is thereby enhanced.

2. *Poise.* As we observed earlier in our comments about the power of suggestion deriving from the speaker's delivery, the speaker who seems to be in command of himself inspires confidence. President Kennedy inspired confidence in his answers to hostile questions, because he never appeared to become unsettled by the hostility.

3. *Modesty.* This trait should not be confused with self-effacement or "false" modesty. In the sense in which we use it here, it suggests the absence of self-congratulation in any form. Genuinely great men don't have to tell others of their greatness. The speaker who takes himself too seriously can only inspire contempt.

4. *Moderation.* We tend to be wary of those who indulge in overstatement, in personal abuse, in unseemly emotional displays. Moderation is usually equated with reasonableness.

5. *Tact.* Closely associated with moderation is tact. It is defined as the ability to deal with others without giving offense.

In application to persuasion, it means such things as disagreeing without being disagreeable, admonishing without scolding, enlightening without insulting the audience's intelligence.

6. *Friendliness.* Good will is contagious. The speaker who shows his listeners that he is well-disposed toward them, even though there may be matters over which they disagree, clears one of the obstacles to persuasion. It is well to remember, however, that a mere *pose* of friendliness can have extremely adverse effects, if the audience detects it as a pose.

7. *Sincerity.* The used car salesman tells the customer, "I'd like to sell you this car, because, quite frankly, I stand to earn a good commission. Furthermore, you stand to get a good car in the process." His candid disclosure of his real motives may well have a disarming effect upon the customer, because we tend to place credence in the remarks of those we regard as sincere and open in their dealings with others. Of all the traits of character, sincerity may well be the most important to persuasion. We will often overlook a man's vices if we know he is not a "phony."

8. *Genuine concern for the listener's welfare.* The speaker who shows that he is motivated by something more than his own personal gain, that he is genuinely concerned for his listeners as well, will more readily receive our confidence than the speaker we suspect of selfish motives. Here again, the concern should be *sincere.*

These, then, are some of the marks of personal credibility. One word of caution is in order. The speaker who wishes to show himself worthy of respect and emulation must not, in the process, place himself beyond the possibility of emulation.

SUMMARY

Persuasion is the art of inducing others to believe, feel, or act in a way that is predetermined by the speaker. Successful persuasion rests upon a thorough knowledge of the audience and its attitude toward the speech topic, the speech purpose, and toward the speaker himself. The common topics of persuasion arise out of questions of policy, questions of fact, and questions of value. The speaker's decision as to what should constitute the precise issue of a persuasive speech should be guided by his knowledge of where the audience is in its thinking about the subject. The modes of persuasion are through logical appeals, through information, through psychological appeals, and through the speaker's personal credibility. The two constituents of logical persuasion are evidence and reasoning. Evidence may be either factual or may be in the form of a statement of opinion. Evidence should be derived from an authoritative source, it should be fairly presented, it should be recent, it should be capable of corroboration. Reasoning takes four forms. Deductive reasoning moves from the general rule or axiom to the specific case at hand. Inductive reasoning proceeds from particular cases to a generalization about all cases. Reasoning from analogy is based on the supposition that because two things are alike in certain known respects they will also be alike in the point at issue. Causal reasoning may appear in at least three forms—from cause-to-effect, from effect-to-cause, or from effect-to-effect.

Persuasion through information is essentially the presentation of evidence without the accompanying inferences that would be used in persuasion through logical appeals. The audience, rather than the speaker, provides the inference.

Persuasion through psychological appeals involves the use of motivation and suggestion. The needs, wants, and desires to which the speaker may link his message are self-preservation, sex attraction, acquisition of property, self-esteem, personal enjoyment, constructiveness, destructiveness, curiosity, imitation, and altruism. Suggestion is the arousal of a response by indirect means. It may operate through channels external to the speaker, through the speaker's delivery, and through the speaker's message.

Persuasion through personal credibility is attained when the speaker manifests poise, modesty, moderation, tact, friendliness, sincerity, and genuine concern for the listener's welfare.

SUGGESTED READINGS

HERBERT I. ABELSON, *Persuasion: How Opinions and Attitudes Are Changed*, (New York: Springer Publishing Company, Inc., 1959).

ELTON ABERNATHY, *The Advocate: A Manual of Persuasion*, (New York: David McKay Co., 1964).

KENNETH ANDERSON, and THEODORE CLEVENGER, JR., "A Summary of Experimental Research in Ethos," *Speech Monographs*, XX, (June, 1963), pp. 59-78.

A. CRAIG BAIRD, and FRANKLIN H. KNOWER, *Essentials of General Speech*, (New York: McGraw-Hill Book Co., Inc., 1952). Chapters 13 and 14.

E. G. BORMANN, "An Empirical Approach to Certain Concepts of Logical Proof," *Central States Speech Journal*, (1961), 85-91.

WINSTON L. BREMBECK, and WILLIAM S. HOWELL, *Persuasion: A Means of Social Control*, (Englewood Cliffs, N. J.: Prentice-Hall, Inc., 1952).

DONALD C. BRYANT, and KARL R. WALLACE, *Fundamentals of Public Speaking*, 3rd edition, (New York: Appleton-Century-Crofts, Inc., 1960). Chapters 17-23.

WILBUR E. GILMAN, BOWER ALY, and HOLLIS L. WHITE, *The Fundamentals of Speaking*, 2nd edition, (New York: The Macmillan Company, 1964). Chapter 3.

CARL I. HOVLAND, IRVING L. JANIS, and HAROLD H. KELLEY, *Communication and Persuasion*, (New Haven: Yale University Press, 1953). Chapter 2.

PATRICK O. MARSH, *Persuasive Speaking, Theory, Models, Practice*, (New York: Harper and Row, 1967).

WAYNE C. MINNICK, *The Art of Persuasion*, (New York: Houghton Mifflin Company, 1957).

ALAN H. MONROE, *Principles and Types of Speech*, 5th edition, (Chicago: Scott, Foresman and Co., 1962). Chapters 10, 16, 21, and 22.

ROBERT T. OLIVER, *The Psychology of Persuasive Speech*, (New York: Longmans, Green, and Company, 1957).

EDWARD ROGGE, and JAMES C. CHING, *Advanced Public Speaking*, (New York: Holt, Rinehart and Winston, Inc., 1966). Chapters 4 and 5.

Harold Sponberg, "The Relative Effectiveness of Climax and Anti-Climax Order in an Argumentative Speech," *Speech Monographs*, No. 1 (1946), pp. 35-44.

Wayne N. Thompson, and Seth A. Fessenden, *Basic Experiences in Speech*, 2nd edition, (Englewood Cliffs, N. J.: Prentice Hall, Inc., 1958). Chapters 10 and 11.

X

INFORMATIVE SPEAKING

BEING UNDERSTOOD

Earlier in the text we noted that one of the primary functions of speech is to provide man with a means of transferring knowledge from person to person and from generation to generation. It shall be our concern now to discuss this vital function of speech—THE PRESENTATION OF INFORMATION IN A FASHION THAT MAKES IT HIGHLY COMPREHENSIBLE.

Situations requiring this type of discourse are numerous. Almost all teaching can be labeled informative speaking. Likewise, the instructions and training given to workmen, office and sales help can be placed in this particular category. Even the directions given by the person telling a friend how to get to Main Street must be labeled informative speaking. At all levels of communication, both formal and informal, informative speaking occurs.

Informative speaking seeks to impart materials that will increase the listener's knowledge of a given subject. If you know a great deal about astronomy and give a speech on the topic, you expect your listeners to know more about the subject when you complete your talk. Therefore, the PRIMARY OB-

JECTIVE OF INFORMATIVE SPEAKING IS TO PRESENT INFORMATION
SO THAT IT WILL BE EASILY UNDERSTOOD AND REMEMBERED BY
YOUR AUDIENCE.

TYPES OF INFORMATIVE SPEECHES

While all informative speeches are alike in that they seek
to give information and increase understanding, they may be
separated into the following basic types: (1) *Descriptions.* You
may wish to describe an individual, a location, an event, a
reaction, or a mood. In each of these instances you are primarily concerned with having the audience see and experience
what you are describing. (2) *Reports.* Book reports, reports
on articles, committee reports, etc., are commonly employed by
the college student. Your responsibility is to transmit accurately
what you have read, discovered, or deliberated upon. (3) *Explanations.* This is a general term for information pertaining
to the operation of a process or the workings of some agent.
In short, you are explaining how something works. (4) *Instructions.* You may wish to tell others how to perform a specific act, such as how to administer first-aid. Employers use
instructions to show new employees how certain tasks are
performed.

STEPS IN PREPARATION

In Chapter I we discussed the six steps of preparation necessary for successful speech making. It was pointed out that before any behavior can be changed, or any response secured, there
must be both analysis and preparation. Much of what we now
say about the speech to increase understanding has already
been examined under other headings. There are, however, some
specific principles of preparing the informative speech that bear
closer examination.

Determining the Purpose and Selecting a Topic

If you are to make ideas clear to an audience, you must
first determine what you want the audience to know about
these ideas at the conclusion of your talk. The specific purpose

of any given informative speech is a statement of *exactly* what
the speaker wants the audience to understand. For example:

1. To have the audience understand how the North Atlantic
   Treaty Organization is financed.
2. To have the audience understand how to analyze dreams.
3. To have the audience understand the workings of a political party convention.
4. To have the audience understand the methods of putting
   a golf ball.

All of these specific purposes tell precisely what it is the
speaker wishes his audience to understand and know.

In choosing and narrowing a topic for the informative speech
you should apply the tests presented earlier in the book. In
substance, you should (1) know more about the topic than do
the members of the audience, (2) be able to locate enough
material, (3) choose something adapted to the listeners (conduct an analysis of the audience and occasion), (4) select a
subject appropriate to the occasion, and (5) select a subject
that interests you.

Gather and Select Materials

If you are to secure understanding your speech must contain the materials that will contribute to clarity and comprehension. As noted earlier, in gathering the data for a talk you
should be adaptable, selective, accurate, objective and thorough.

In order to accomplish these objectives you should begin
by making an inventory of what you already know and the
material you have available to you. You will then be in a
position to determine what additional materials you need. After
the inventory, you are ready to locate and gather the necessary
information. By realizing your aims, personal resources and
limitations, you can select the illustrations, examples, comparisons, definitions, statistical data, interest factors, forms of restatement, and the visual aids that will accomplish your specific purpose.

It should be underscored once again that an effective speaker
gathers more material than he will be able to use. A thorough
preparation and analysis will make you more knowledgeable

about the topic and enable you to be more selective as to what you include and what you omit.

THE MATERIALS OF INFORMATIVE SPEAKING

Clarity, understanding and interest are the key elements found in successful informative speaking. The student of communication will discover that these elements are attainable through careful application of the following techniques and principles of effective exposition.

Definition

Mistakes are often made because people are confused about meanings. Because the speaker is usually very familiar with the subject matter he is discussing, he may forget to define some of the basic and important terms, phrases or concepts. In addition, because words are simply symbols, and usually interpreted differently by different people, listeners can become confused by the meanings of various words.

In defining words, phrases or abstract ideas the speaker should try to observe the following rules: (1) Define the unknown in terms of the known. Make a statement or use an illustration with which the audience is familiar. Then, through comparison proceed to the unknown. Using language that is simpler than the original expression is another application of this principle. Going from the known to the unknown establishes a common frame of reference and allows the audience to see what you mean. For example, a veteran Navy radarman defined radar by comparing it to the action of a tennis ball being bounced off a garage door. (2) Define the word by placing it in the context in which it will be used; for example, you might say, "In discussing the problem of school drop-outs we shall concern ourselves with the student who leaves school, for whatever reason, before graduation or before the age of 18." In this way the audience knows who you are talking about when you use the term "drop-out." (3) Try to anticipate the knowledge level of your audience on the particular topic so that you will be in a position to decide which words need defining. If you were talking to a group of electronics experts and used the simple radar analogy cited above you might find that you had insulted their egos, yet the same radar analogy might be very effective for a group of liberal arts majors.

Examples

The technique of example, which was explained in detail in Chapter V, is perhaps the simplest and the most common of the devices of informative speaking. Its success depends upon four factors: (1) The example should be brief and pointed. (2) It should be relevant to whatever the speaker is explaining. (3) It should be adapted to the educational and interest level of the audience. (4) It should be consistent with the tone of the speech and not appear to be something the speaker has just added for no apparent reason.

An example may be either a specific instance or a detailed illustration, and can appear as real or fictitious, in verbal form or in graphic form. In a speech on water pollution you might employ a graphic example by showing a large picture of some of the foreign matter found in many of our rivers and streams. The important criterion is that it prove or clarify the generalization being made. For instance, if you were speaking on the various funeral customs in Africa, you might offer the listener two or three factual examples of the rituals performed by some of the tribes. This would explain your point in a vivid and concrete form while holding the attention of your listeners.

Comparisons and Contrasts

Clarity may be enhanced and interest maintained through the use of comparison and contrast. Comparison shows how two things are alike while contrast points out the way in which they differ. These devices are useful in that they lead the listener from the known to the unknown. In explaining the functions of the United States Senate you might use comparison by explaining the relationship between the Senate and your college's Student Council. By pointing out the duties and functions of the Council (known) you would show the likeness in the Senate (unknown). Analogy is often a good form of comparison in that it also attempts to compare the known with the unknown.

Statistics

It is frequently useful to explain an idea in terms of size or quantity. For example, if you were talking about income tax in the United States it would be helpful to offer some statistics on the various programs and the numerous methods of calculating percentages.

In using statistics a few rules and guides should be kept in mind. By themselves statistics are abstract and meaningless. To be useful they must be compared or contrasted with something else to show how many, how few, how large or how small the idea or thing really is. If you were going to offer statistics dealing with the number of light-years to the nearest star you might make such figures meaningful by explaining a light-year in terms of how many trips that would involve between the campus and the downtown area. Second, a large list of numbers is hard to comprehend. Therefore, whenever possible try to use round numbers. Third, it is important that you be very selective in citing statistics, for a listener will tire of a lengthy discussion of facts and figures. Fourth, see that your statistics meet the tests advanced in Chapter V. Whether your aim be informative or persuasive your material should be authentic, complete and clear.

Description

There will be occasions when description will be the best method of explaining and clarifying the thought you are trying to develop. In description the speaker pictures or portrays an object, event or person by stimulating the listener's sense of sight, sound, smell, taste or feeling. The listeners mind is focused on the object by means of vivid word pictures. A speech on California National Forests might well employ descriptions of the wildlife, water sources, and vegetation that constitute the elements of the forest.

Partition, Enumeration and Summary

Memory is short, and as the speaker moves through his speech we frequently lose track of his main thesis. It is therefore of prime importance that a speaker employ as many devices as he can that will aid the listener in remembering the main ideas as they are developed throughout the talk. PARTITION, ENUMERATION and SUMMARY are three such techniques that contribute to this increased understanding and retention.

A PARTITION (often referred to as an initial summary or "preview") is a list offered early in the speech of the points that will be covered. In short, you simply tell your audience what main ideas you plan to treat in the body of your speech. For example, "In talking about how to insulate a room I shall first of all take up the procedures for insulating the floor, then those for insulating the walls, and finally the procedures for insulating the ceiling." Having highlighted what you plan to cover, you are now ready to move to the body of your talk.

ENUMERATION, which occurs during the body of your speech, is the numbering of each point as it is introduced. "First . . ., Second . . ., and Third . . ." This technique is helpful in increasing clarity in that it alerts the audience to movements from one idea to another.

SUMMARY is the reiteration of the main items at the close of the entire speech. For example, "In insulating a room we looked at the techniques used for insulating the floor, the wall and the ceiling."

RESTATEMENT and REPETITION are two methods of using both internal and final summaries in such a way as to reinforce learning and promote interest. RESTATEMENT uses new words to convey and echo an idea already discussed in a speech. After giving a speech on "The Dangers of Cigarette Smoking" you might want to restate your main thesis to "cigarette smoking can cause you great physical harm." In this way the listeners hear the idea again, but expressed this time in a new manner. REPETITION is the use of identical wording to repeat the idea. By repeating the main point it is better remembered. Both restatement and repetition have their roots in learning theory and should be used frequently in communication.

ORGANIZING THE SPEECH TO INFORM

Systematic arrangement of material is crucial in informative speaking if the listener is to retain the information presented. Listen carefully the next time you hear an informative talk and you will discover that there are occasions when the educated as well as the uneducated forget the importance of organization and clarity. Speeches that seem to leap from point to point without offering any internal or external clue will seldom leave the listener with anything meaningful.

The Introduction

The dual purposes of any introduction are to alert the audience to the main subject of the speech and to arouse in the listener a desire for the detailed information contained in the body of the speech.

Specific methods of starting a speech were discussed in detail in Chapter VI. The selection of a method will be determined by factors relating to the topic, audience interest, audience knowledge level, speaking-time available, and the speaking occasion. When listeners are not vitally concerned with the topic it is often quite profitable to begin with a rhetorical question, startling statement, or unusual illustration. These devices often arouse the apathetic and disinterested listener.

In all communication situations it is to your advantage if you can stimulate a desire on the part of the audience to want to listen to your presentation. In the introduction to the informative speech make it clear to your audience that your topic holds significance for them and that they will benefit by listening. You can better hold attention during the body of your speech if you have already created an atmosphere of curiosity and interest. By motivating the audience early in the speech you also increase the probability that they will learn something by the conclusion of your talk.

In your introduction you should also provide a brief initial summary (preview) of the main points to be taken up in the body of your speech. By telling your audience that your speech on the subject of "How to Swing a Golf Club" will deal with the grip, the stance and the swing, you are allowing them a glimpse of your organizational pattern as a means of making their job of listening easier. You are preparing them for what is coming, and they will find it much simpler to locate your main ideas.

The Body

Since the introduction has (1) captured the listener's attention, (2) aroused his interest in the information to come, and (3) previewed your main points, you are ready to present the information itself. To promote the listener's comprehension of your ideas, and to maintain his attention at a high level, you should organize the body of your speech into meaningful groupings. The division of the whole into its parts is an essential step in explaining any complex machine, process or concept. No one, for example, can understand all aspects of public welfare, but most people could assimilate certain features if they were presented and explained separately. In most instances the classification and division of the speech is inevitable in light of the subject matter. These groupings will be more easily remembered if they can be worded into a logical pattern. Let us reexamine some of the patterns of arrangement discussed in Chapter VI in light of their application to informative speaking.

CHRONOLOGICAL PATTERN

The chronological, or time pattern, has its greatest value in explanations of processes, in presentation of historic events, and in relating personal experiences. In discussing "The History of Air Travel" you might develop your material under three headings:

    I. Early attempts at flying.

    II. Air travel today.

    III. The future of air travel.

When giving a speech on "The Legislative Process" the order might well be:

I. Drafting a bill.
II. Committee hearings.
III. Debate on the floor of Congress.

SPATIAL PATTERN

Use of spatial order is especially effective in speeches describing a scene, a location, or a geographical distribution. For instance, the body of your speech could be arranged from North to South, from top to bottom, or from center to outside. In talking on the topic of "Violence in the United States," your order might be:

I. Violence on the East Coast.
II. Violence in the Middle West.
III. Violence on the West Coast.

For a speech on "The Life Under the Sea" you might select the following order:

I. Surface sea life.
II. Sea life twenty feet below the ocean.
III. Sea life on the ocean floor.

CAUSAL ORDER

In using the causal order you may tell of the causes of certain effects, or, tell of the effects resulting from various causes. In giving a talk on "The Sun and the Individual," your pattern might appear:

I. The effects of the sun on the skin.
II. The effects of the sun on the eyes.
III. The effects of the sun on the hair.

When treating the topic "Why World War II?" you might select the following arrangement:

I. United States and German relations before 1941.
II. United States and Italian relations before 1941.
III. United States and Japanese relations before 1941.

By examining the relationship of the United States to each of these countries one is able to point out possible causes for World War II.

TOPICAL PATTERN

The topical pattern is probably the most frequently used of all patterns. This arrangement sets out several facets of a topic that are obviously related and consistent. If you are talking about "The Financial Structure of a Major Company," your pattern might include:

    I.   The company's assets.
    II. The company's liabilities.
    III. The company's endowments.

The key to the topical pattern is that the arrangement is rather apparent and the one that an audience most likely expects.

The speaker may wish to order his material so that it moves from the simplest to the most complex, the most familiar to the least familiar, the least important to the most important, or the most acceptable to the least acceptable.

During the body of the speech the speaker should remember to hold the audience's attention. Too often speakers only concentrate on securing attention at the beginning of their talk, and forget that there is a limit to any person's capacity for attending to and absorbing facts. The speaker delivering an informative speech must therefore make effective and liberal use of humor, vivid language, suspense, analogy, and the interest and attention devices discussed in Chapter VII.

Finally, the speaker should also keep in mind the importance of using concrete data. We have already cautioned that the successful communicator is not abstract, vague, or general, but offers information and material that is clear, specific, accurate, and appropriate. In informative speaking, when the response sought is understanding, it behooves the speaker to use concrete data. An audience would have a difficult time remembering very much about a speech that tried to explain the entire subject of "Mental Health" in ten minutes. There simply wouldn't be time to supply the needed data to make the subject meaningful.

The Conclusion

Methods of concluding a speech were explained in some detail in Chapter VI and can profitably be reviewed as part of your training for informative speaking. There are, however, certain techniques of concluding that are especially valuable for the speech to inform. For example, it may be helpful to re-state your main message and summarize its main points. You may desire to heighten audience interest once again and sug-gest areas where they will be able to add to or clarify some concepts you mentioned.

The most popular concluding technique is the final sum-mary (or reiteration). People tend to pay close attention when they feel the end of the speech is near. The final summary takes advantage of this captured attention by reviewing the main ideas in the *same* order they were presented in the initial summary and in the body of the speech. In speaking on the topic of "College Registration," one might conclude by saying, "So we have seen that you can register for classes in three ways. First, you can register by mail; second, you can make special arrangements with the specific instructors; and finally, you can sign up in the Registration office on the first day of classes."

VISUAL AIDS

The value of visual aids as a means of support was sug-gested in Chapter V when we discussed the forms of support. Visual aids are useful in informative discourse in that they make ideas more vivid, more lasting, and more understandable. Visual aids are helpful in clarifying new terms or ideas which are not readily understood or meaningful to many in the audience. The word "larynx" might be unfamiliar to the listeners, but a model or diagram would quickly offer the audience a definition of the term, "steam generating plan" would be more meaningful when accompanied by a diagram, and "player protection gear" would be clarified by a display of a football player's shoulder pads, hip pads, and helmet. A common principle of learning maintains that it is worthwhile to employ as many senses as possible, that the more associations a person has with an idea the better are his chances of remembering it. Being able to see the idea, as well as hear it, contributes to both of these objectives. We have stressed throughout this chapter the importance of interest and attention as part of the informative process. A pretty picture, a shiny object, or a drawing provides the listener with an object upon which he can focus his attention, and he is usually anxious to hear what the speaker has to say about it.

Types of Visual Aids

1. *Specimens and models.* Objects taken from their natural settings or models and mock-ups of actual objects can be quite helpful in securing understanding of an idea. Seeing a disassembled model of a nuclear submarine would be very helpful to a speaker trying to explain the operation of the *U. S. S. Nautilus.* If at all possible, the use of the actual object is suggested, because *reality* is more compelling than a mere representation of reality.

2. *Charts and graphs.* Abstract or complicated ideas can often be made more understandable through use of charts and graphs. The increase in personal income taxes over the last twenty years can be well illustrated on a graph that shows, on the vertical axis, the years involved and, on the horizontal axis, the average amount of taxes paid by each individual. The five most common graphs and charts are: (a) the TREE chart, which normally reveals the simple beginning of an idea or process and carries it on to more detailed stages of development; (b) the ORGANIZATIONAL chart, which shows, by means of blocks and interconnecting lines, the hierarchy of control and responsibility; (c) the COMPARISON chart, which compares or contrasts two or more quantities, usually of a statistical nature, in terms of each other or in terms of other predetermined quantities; (d) the "PIE-GRAPH," which is a circle divided into several pie-shaped segments, each segment representing a classified item and its relationship to the other items; (e) the BAR graph and the LINE graph, which are usually employed to represent trends, as in a sales graph.

3. *Posters, cartoons, pictures and photographs* also are quite useful in both clarifying ideas and holding the interest of the audience.

Using Visual Aids

By following some simple guide lines in the use of visual aids you will discover that your material will be clearer, more meaningful and more interesting.

1. In preparing and selecting your visual aid make certain that the aid is pertinent to the subject and serves a real purpose.

2. The material on the visual aid should be completely accurate in both representation and authenticity. This does not mean that some forms of exaggeration can not be used to show emphasis.

3. The visual aid should not contain any distracting elements. For example, non-essential details or details that are so poorly depicted that they can't be accurately interpreted may well obscure rather than clarify your ideas.

4. In most instances it is best to display only one visual aid at a time. To have more than one aid in front of the audience at one time encourages the listeners to divide their attention between the aids and perhaps miss certain important points about the one you happen to be discussing.

5. See that the lettering, art work, or other main features are large enough and clear enough and of sufficient contrast for all viewers to see.

6. Remember the necessity for eye contact and speak to the *audience*—not to the visual aid.

7. Be sure to coordinate your visual aid with your words. Don't point to a wheel of a car when you are talking about the fenders, or show one aid while talking about something shown by another.

8. Check the physical surroundings and furnishings so that you will not discover, when it is too late, that there is no place to put your chart, or no electrical outlet available for your tape recorder. Many speakers have found they have had to hold their aids throughout their talks because they failed to investigate the accommodations available.

9. Distributing any material to your audience during the speech should, as a rule, be avoided. The circulating material offers the listener an easy excuse to stop listening. If you must distribute material, be sure to give it to every person in your audience. Trying to read over someone's shoulder can cause confusion in the audience.

SUMMARY

The principles of communication discussed throughout this book are directly applicable to informative speaking. There are, however, certain steps that must be applied when sending someone a message intended to increase his knowledge of a particular subject. In outline form, these steps are:

I. Introduction
   A. Arouse attention.
   B. Stimulate interest.
   C. Summarize the main points to be covered in the speech.

II. Body
   A. Adapt material to the audience—audience analysis.
   B. Employ clear organization.
   C. Explain the unknown in terms of the known.
   D. Use concrete and specific information.
   E. Dramatize the main points.
   F. Use factors of interest and attention.
   G. Make use of repetition and restatement.
   H. Use effective visual aids.

III. Conclusion
   A. Present summary of the main points.
   B. Arouse interest in further investigation.

SUGGESTED READINGS

JOHN W. BLACK, "Speech Intelligibility: A Summary of Recent Research," *Journal of Communication*, XL, (June, 1961). pp. 87-94.

ROBERT D. BROWN, and DAVID G. SPENCER, eds., *Exposition and Persuasion*, (New York: Appleton-Century-Crofts, Inc., 1957). Part I and II.

HERBERT HACKETT, MARTIN ANDERSEN, SETH FESSENDEN, and LESSIE LEE HAGEN, *Understanding and Being Understood*, (New York: Longmans, Green and Company, 1957). Chapter 24.

S. I. HAYAKAWA, *Language in Action: A Guide to Accurate Thinking*, (New York: Harcourt, Brace and World, Inc., 1940). Chapter 3.

EDWARD ROGGE, and JAMES C. CHING, *Advanced Public Speaking*, (New York: Holt, Rinehart and Winston, Inc., 1966). Chapters 12-14.

Wesley A. Wiksell, *Do They Understand You?* (New York: The Macmillan Company, 1960). Part 4.

Walter Wittich, and Charles F. Schuller, *Audio-Visual Materials: Their Nature and Use*, (New York: Harper and Brothers, 1953). Chapters 4 and 5.

XI

SPECIAL OCCASIONS

THE UNIQUE COMMUNICATION SITUATION

Most occasions for public or private discourse call for speeches whose primary purposes are to inform or persuade. The principles and techniques of informing and persuading are basically the same regardless of the occasion which dictates the speech. That is to say, introduction, body and conclusion, evidence, attention, interest, organization, delivery, motivation, and language are common to *all* speaking situations. There are occasions, however, when the situation demands an extension or combination of the basic elements found in informing and persuading. Knowing that all forms of communication have a great deal in common, the trained and conscientious speaker can quickly adapt his skills to the unique and different situation.

No list or treatment of special occasions could ever be complete, for in one sense each communication situation and occasion is novel and original. Yet there are some very specific occasions that the speaker may find himself in as he moves from environment to environment. It is on these occasions that the speaker must remember all of his past speech training at the same time he is utilizing the items that relate directly to the special occasion. In this final chapter we will examine some of these common types and forms of discourse and deliberation.

We have selected the entertaining speech, the after-dinner speech, the impromptu speech, the introduction speech and group discussion to treat in some detail, for it is these forms of discourse and deliberation that you are most likely to encounter.

THE ENTERTAINING SPEECH

All speeches, to some extent, may entertain the listener. Yet there are specific occasions when the objective is not to increase someone's knowledge or even change the destiny of civilization, but rather to have the audience relax in a light-hearted mood and in an enjoyable atmosphere. In short, the only purpose of this type of speech is entertainment—everything else must be subordinated.

Characteristics of Entertaining

The speech to entertain may well show itself as a humorous talk, but all speeches to entertain need not be funny. The one basic requirement for all speeches of ENTERTAINMENT is that THEY MUST HOLD ATTENTION AND INTEREST IN THEMSELVES. The speaker can best accomplish this objective by having his speech include many of the factors of attention and interest discussed in Chapter VII. Novelty and suspense are two of the factors that are often employed.

The dominant characteristics of the speech to entertain are as follows:

1. In presenting the speech to entertain *the delivery should be lively, enthusiastic, and animated.* In most instances the speech is delivered extemporaneously, so that a spontaneous and natural effect will be produced.

2. *Stories, illustrations, and humorous anecdotes are liberally used* in this type of speech. The fully-developed example is often so vivid and real it serves to capture and maintain attention. Remember, these illustrations should be fresh and original and free from any appearance of triteness. Furthermore, "canned" illustrations and anecdotes should be avoided.

3. The speech to entertain, like all speeches, is *well organized and easy to follow, and is normally constructed around a central theme or idea.* The theme for the speech to entertain should be appropriate to the audience and occasion. In many instances it may deal with a common topic in a unique and different manner, such as the problems of eating three meals a day while orbiting the earth in a space capsule.

4. *The response sought by the speaker who is entertaining is immediate and momentary.* The audience may remember some of the information long after the speech, but the speaker's primary concern is the covert or overt behavior *at the time* of the talk.

The Use of Humor

Humor is indeed the most common ingredient found in the speech to entertain. It holds our attention and, if used correctly, creates an enjoyable and friendly atmosphere. The problem of what constitutes humor has been discussed for centuries. People have long asked, what makes us laugh? Several of the more common aspects of pleasure and enjoyment will be examined at this time as a means of trying to supply the speaker with some guidelines in his selection and use of humor.

Exaggeration

Take a possible occurrence, make it larger and overstate it, and you have a potential humorous situation. As long as the exaggeration has a touch of reality we can enjoy its obvious distortion. In a play called *The Miser* exaggeration is used as humor when someone talks of the miser who is so cheap he steals oats from his own livestock. Another example of exaggeration is the speaker who tells the audience that the traffic problem is so bad that he has had to equip his car with a three day supply of food in case he decides to use the freeway.

Incongruity

In a very real sense incongruity consists of any situation in which the parts do not fit together. The unusual, the sudden and unexpected twist, and the inconsistency are all potential sources of humor. An example of incongruity would be the story of the teen-age boy who is upset because his parents won't let him borrow *their* hot rod, surfboard or rock-and-roll records. Here we have an incongruous situation—parents with teen-age toys.

Attacking Authority

We all know how much we enjoy seeing the boss, the sergeant, the policeman or some other figure of authority having fun poked at him. Even the mother-in-law jokes are instances of having fun at the expense of someone or something that is normally regarded reverently. In poking fun at others it is always important to use good taste and not offend anyone's morals or standards.

There are many other devices that lend themselves to humor. For example, *the pun, irony, sarcasm,* and *burlesque* can all be effectively used. Yet the greatest source of humor comes from the creative and imaginative work all of us do when we sit and reflect. In short, *thinking* about what is humorous usually produces some excellent and rewarding examples and situations.

DEVELOPING THE SPEECH

A primary consideration in the development of the speech to entertain is your knowing the exact makeup of the audience. In addition, your audience analysis should include some information on the occasion. It is important to know if the audience came only to listen to you, to laugh, or if they expect some concrete information to take home. Once these questions have been answered you are ready to determine your central theme, decide upon an introduction, an organizational pattern for the body, and your conclusion.

Introduction

The opening remarks in the speech to entertain, have the task of arousing attention, setting the mood, and establishing the main point. In the speech to entertain the speaker must make it quite clear that he does not plan to develop any profound concepts, for if the audience expects him to "get somewhere" they will be confused as he continues to provide only entertainment. If you return to Chapter VI, you will find a discussion of some of the methods that can be used in starting the speech to entertain. The illustration is a very popular opening device in entertaining.

Body

The topical order or the chronological order best serve the objectives of entertaining although the speaker can use any of the other organizational patterns treated in Chapter VI. The entertaining speech can also be organized around a simple, long narrative, a series of short narratives with a theme, or by developing satire or exaggeration. In any case, the speech to entertain must not lead off in many different directions, but rather it should be built around a central theme with natural transitions.

Conclusion

The conclusion is usually very brief and continues to carry forth the general mood. The devices for concluding were discussed in Chapter VI, and should be reviewed as a means of determining which technique best applies to the specific communication situation the speaker faces.

THE AFTER-DINNER SPEECH

The after-dinner speech, which is, in many instances, considered a speech to entertain, is perhaps the most widely used occasional speech. It should be stressed, however, that many speeches that take place after a meal may be very serious and vital. Yet there seems to be a tradition that seeks to establish a relaxed and friendly atmosphere after a meal. In these cases THE AFTER-DINNER SPEECH IS CHARACTERIZED BY A SHORT, GENIAL AND HUMOROUS TALK. Because of its relationship to the speech to entertain, the after-dinner speaker should heed the advice offered those who seek to deliver the entertaining speech.

There are a few special considerations to keep in mind as one prepares and delivers an after-dinner talk.

1. After having enjoyed a meal and conversation with friends, an audience is normally in a good mood by the time the after-dinner speaker begins his talk. In most instances, because this friendly atmosphere prevails, the speaker should try to be optimistic and good-humored. Pessimism, bitterness, gloom and denunciation make a poor combination with a full stomach. Therefore, the selection of an appropriate topic is essential in after-dinner speaking. This, in turn, puts an added emphasis on audience analysis. A story or a joke that is funny to one group of individuals may fail to arouse even a smile from another group.

2. The relationship between speaker and audience in the after-dinner situation should be more informal than formal in its organization, language and delivery.

3. The after-dinner talk is normally quite brief. Attention spans grow short after a pleasant meal.

4. The material should be interesting and easy to understand. Humor, interesting stories, examples, and unique experiences are at the root of after-dinner speaking.

5. Most after-dinner speeches are well prepared. The speaker does not have to hesitate or grope for his ideas or words. The speaker must be careful not to let this thoroughness of preparation be carried to the extent that he loses spontaneity and thus destroys the friendly and casual mood essential to effective after-dinner speaking.

THE IMPROMPTU SPEECH

There will be occasions when you are called upon to deliver an offhand response to a demand or a request for a "few remarks" on a specific subject. The IMPROMPTU (or spur-of-the-moment-) speech is delivered in just such a situation. It is a speech that simply cannot be thoroughly prepared. We see this type of speaking every day. In discussions, in meetings, at conferences, in classes and in conversation, we are asked to give our ideas and opinions on countless subjects. Because of the lack of immediate preparation, many view impromptu speaking as the most difficult of all speech forms. If one can learn to remain calm when called upon to give a talk, he will discover that the impromptu situation is not nearly as menacing as first anticipated.

The trained speaker soon strikes upon the idea that there are three different times when he can prepare for the impromptu speech. First, if one is fortunate enough to possess a large storehouse of information, he can usually find something worthwhile to say. A broad background of reading and experience are invaluable in meeting the challenge of impromptu speaking. As we pointed out earlier in the text, an alert individual is constantly preparing for a speech. Second, if one suspects that he might be called upon he can pay close attention to what is going on at the meeting and what is being said at the platform. By observing what is going on you may be able to think about what you would say if called upon. Third, one can learn to utilize the brief period between the time he is called upon and the time he has to utter his first words. Although this period of time may range from a few seconds to a few minutes, it can still be put to good use.

The following suggestions, if practiced, will help the speaker overcome his fears, and will also aid him in accomplishing his purpose.

1. *Listening* is the first step in preparing an impromptu speech. You will discover that what was said or what happened just before your speech can serve as the main point of your message. If you are daydreaming instead of listening, you may find yourself red-faced and trembling. In short, when called upon to speak try to utilize and develop what has been said; to do this you must pay attention.

2. Try to decide on an approach to the topic *before* you begin to speak. Some common techniques are to agree or disagree with the issue in question, ask the audience to do something, or highlight the truth or falsehood of the statement or idea. In all cases it is best to develop only one point or idea.

3. Select an organizational plan that will let you develop your main point. Here are a few of the more frequent patterns:

    a. Refer to what has been said by a previous speaker.

       State your position on the issue.

> Develop your position by illustration, analogy, or any appropriate form of support.
> b. Tell the audience what you plan to do.
> Tell them why it is important.
> Carry out your plan.
> c. Start with an illustration.
> Explain how it proves or clarifies your point.

4. Remember that the impromptu speech, although it lacks detailed preparation, it should still contain the ingredients of any successful speech. For example, the introduction, interest and attention factors, motive appeals, concrete language, forms of support, a conclusion, and the like should be included in the impromptu speech.

5. The ability to prepare and deliver an impromptu speech can be greatly improved if one is willing to practice. As you practice this type of speaking you will discover that your nervousness decreases. As you gain confidence from practice you will also face the realization that speaking on the spur-of-the-moment is really something quite easy and something you do each day.

Listed below are some topics, as well as some sentences, that can be used to practice impromptu speaking.

1.	Optimism	11.	Faces
2.	Secrets	12.	Immortality
3.	Philanthropy	13.	Progress
4.	Rudeness	14.	Individuality
5.	Enemies	15.	Conscience
6.	Manners	16.	Cheating
7.	Tragedy	17.	Drama
8.	Socialism	18.	Fear
9.	Anarchy	19.	Prejudice
10.	Chivalry	20.	Hobbies

a. My first automobile.
b. The divorce problem in the United States.
c. The small college vs. the large university.
d. The dangers of "managed-news."
e. The state of today's young people.
f. My greatest disappointment.
g. Improving my college's image.
h. The impact of the communication explosion.

    i. "The war to end wars."
    j. "The war to end us all."
    k. What about capital punishment?
    l. Waste in government.
    m. What is a liberal education?
    n. Our role in South America.
    o. One answer to over-population.
    p. What is modern religion?
    q. The influence of Madison Avenue.
    r. The limits of free speech.
    s. The need for a good vocabulary.
    t. How successful is the United Nations?

MAKING INTRODUCTIONS

A SPEECH OF INTRODUCTION is another common type of occasional speaking, yet it is one that is often poorly done. People often forget that the introduction serves to link the guest speaker with the audience. It should not be used to demonstrate the introducer's cleverness or "superior knowledge."

The introduction has two main purposes. First, it should acquaint the audience with the guest speaker, and, second, it should arouse interest in the talk. In order to see to it that the speaker and his speech secure a favorable reception the introducer can follow a few simple rules.

1. *Be brief.* As noted earlier, the introducer subordinates his own speech for the sake of the main talk. In most instances, thirty seconds to two minutes is normally the time allotted to the person making the introduction.

2. In planning your introduction see to it that your information concerning the speaker, his background and his topic, *is accurate.* Errors in pronunciation, particularly of the speaker's name or personal data, can cause a great deal of embarrassment to you, the speaker, and the audience. It is worthwhile to secure the essential and personal information from the speaker himself well in advance of your formal introduction.

3. It is often quite effective if you can begin the introduction with a brief reference to the nature of the occasion. This may well serve as a bond between the speaker and the listeners. There may also be occasions where it will be of value to emphasize the importance of the subject.

4. Once you have established rapport with the audience, by humor, reference to occasion, or by some other form of motivation, you are ready to give the biographical data necessary to identify the speaker and to make him sound interesting and authoritative to the audience. In most cases the biography should include: (a) where he lives, (b) his achievements (publications, honors and awards, etc.), (c) his background on the topic (professional and educational), (d) his relationship to the audience, (e) and the reason he was selected to deliver the talk.

5. If the occasion allows for it, you should try to hold off the speaker's full name and/or subject until the end. In this way his name and topic can be presented as a climax.

6. Avoid hackneyed words and phrases. Introductions such as "Our speaker needs no introduction . . ." and "without further ado . . ." are much too common.

7. Pay close attention to the speech so that at the close of the address you can make reference to the ideas and their value to the audience as you thank the speaker.

TAKING PART IN DISCUSSION

You have probably already discovered that there are many communication situations that call for a *sharing* of ideas and a willingness to "talk things over." Whether it be in business, at school, at church, or at social functions, we are constantly having to get together with other individuals in order to discuss items of business or solve mutual problems. When you engage in a situation that brings you face-to-face with others you should be aware of the influence of communication upon the final outcome of the meeting. Being able to communicate effectively on these occasions can make the difference between an "aimless bull session" or a productive communication experience.

The concept of group thinking is fundamental to the democratic process for a number of reasons. In a democratic society it is only natural that decisions should be made after considerable deliberation and discussion. We pride ourselves on being fair—that various points of view are presented and considered before judgement is given or a decision rendered. We maintain, as part of our democratic philosophy, that each person counts and has both the right and the responsibility to contribute to the resolution of his and the public's problems. Group discussion affords the individual an opportunity to conduct his social, political and vocational affairs in a democratic manner, utilizing maximum participation of other trained and interested citizens. In short, we can say that DISCUSSION IS THE SYSTEMATIC AND OBJECTIVE SHARING OF IDEAS AND INFORMATION BY TWO OR MORE PERSONS WHO WORK TOGETHER IN AN EFFORT TO SOLVE A PROBLEM OR TO GAIN A BETTER UNDERSTANDING OF A PROBLEM.

Types of Discussion

Traditionally people have tried to classify various types and forms of group discussion. These classifications are not hard and fast, for in many instances one form may overlap another.

1. *Lecture-forum.* This is the simplest form of public group discussion. A speaker addresses the audience. He is the speaker of the evening—the lecturer. After his speech the lecturer is expected to answer questions directed to him by members of the audience. The audience may contribute opinions of their own during this period. Hence, we have discussion—ideas are being exchanged. Normally there is a chairman to introduce the speaker and to guide the discussion period.

2. *Symposium.* In the symposium each of several speakers, generally two to five, delivers a talk. These speeches center around one topic, theme or issue. Each speaker may explain his position and thoughts on the subject as a whole, or he may be limited to a specific phase of the subject. Frequently the audience is allowed the privilege of asking questions at the conclusion of all of the talks.

3. *Panel.* During the last few years the panel has become a very popular method of group discussion. In a very general sense, a panel is a discussion within a discussion. In this arrangement a limited number of persons, usually four to seven, sit before the audience and discuss a given topic. There are no

planned and set speeches; all the remarks are short and spontaneous. When the panel finishes its discussion there are normally questions from the floor which are answered by the panel members.

4. *Informal group discussion (round-table)*. This is the most common of all the forms of discussion. It is normally a non-audience type of discussion and tends to be more informal than the other methods. It consists of a small group seated around a table. In this setting they exchange their views and their information in a spontaneous and free manner. The stimulus-response pattern is constantly changing as attention is directed from one person to another. This type of pattern is well suited for either decision-making or information-sharing, and is the type of discussion situation in which we most often find ourselves.

Preparing for Discussion

Discussion will be an aimless, purposeless activity if the participants engage in conversation without preparation and forethought. The steps in preparing for discussion involve three closely related activities—selecting a subject, wording a subject, and gathering material.

Selecting the Subject

On most occasions the members of a private discussion group will be in a position to select their own subjects. In deciding what to talk about, and what problem to investigate, the participants will find it helpful to follow a few guidelines.

1. Select problems in which the participants have an interest. If the members of the group feel personally involved they will be far more active in both research and participation. There is ample experimental evidence to point out that we tend to work harder for those causes we feel most strongly about. In addition, we seem to enjoy the experience with added enthusiasm if we are sincerely committed.

2. The topic should be important and worth discussing. Time is too precious and serious questions too numerous to waste time on trivial and frivolous matters.

3. Choose a topic on which ample resource material is available. Sitting around and offering information from the "top of our heads" will result in a "pooling of ignorance."

4. Problems should be selected that can be investigated prior to the discussion and that can be discussed in the time allotted to the group. A group that is rushed, both before and during the discussion, will usually produce a solution that reflects just such a hasty analysis and lack of deliberation.

Wording the Subject

The correct wording and statement of the problem area is as important as the problem itself. For if the group formulates the problem in a way that distorts the real issue, confusion and misunderstanding will result. In addition, the general subject area must be worded into a workable topic if all members of the group are to deal with the same problem. The student of discussion might well consider some of the following suggestions for wording the subject.

1. The subject-problem should be phrased as a question. The question highlights a specific problem while it motivates persons to seek answers to the problem. Phrasing such as "Price fixing" and "War and Peace" are so general and vague that they cannot be discussed in a specific manner. On the other hand, a question such as "What should be the economic role of the United States in Germany?" calls for an answer—hence discussion can take place.

2. The question should be clearly phrased. If the wording is ambiguous, the group may have to spend long periods of time trying to decide what to talk about. A question such as "What should be the current status of business?" is an example of ambiguity. The group must stop and decide what "business" and "current status" mean before they can even start working on the problem. Careful wording of the problem, even before the group begins discussing, also serves the dual role of limiting and restricting the scope of the problem. A topic worded "What are the graduate fellowships offered at San Diego State College?" indicates precisely what the group will talk about.

3. Whenever possible avoid wording the problem-question in a "yes-or-no" form. The "yes-or-no" response limits the avail-

able solutions and also leads to debate instead of cooperation. Questions such as "Should our school adopt a year-round session?" places restrictions on the group and limits the responses the participants can make.

Gathering Material

The amount and depth of preparation in discussion is as vital as in preparing for a speech. If the participants are ill-informed and poorly researched, very little productive deliberation can take place. Each member of a group depends on the other members for different and fresh ideas; if one member fails to gather specific and concrete data the entire group suffers.

We have already written about the processes of gathering and preparing material. The same principles apply to discussion: (1) think carefully on the subject before you start your research; (2) decide what you already know on the subject and what you must research further; (3) gather the additional information you need; (4) accurately record your findings; and (5) organize your material around a purposeful and meaningful pattern.

The Organizational Pattern in Discussion—
Steps in Reflective Thinking

Earlier we mentioned the importance of organization and its role in successful communication. We noted that a speaker needed direction, and if this direction was logical he could not afford the luxury of lengthy digressions and aimless ramblings. The same is true of group discussion. The importance of organization is underscored by the fact that group discussion is conducted through cooperative conversation, with all participants talking about the same subject. In short, THINKING TOGETHER, IN AN ORGANIZED MANNER, THE MEMBERS OF A GROUP SEEK TO SOLVE MUTUAL PROBLEMS.

In most instances group discussion follows the steps of problem-solving developed by John Dewey, American philosopher and educator. Dewey developed a simple pattern that allows the discussants to adapt the steps of problem-solving to group deliberation. These are, briefly, (1) recognition of the problem, (2) description of the problem, (3) discovery of possible solutions, (4) evaluation of solutions and acceptance of the best solution, and (5) plan of action for the preferred solution.

RECOGNITION OF THE PROBLEM

Before one can solve a problem he must be aware of the fact that a problem exists. Therefore, the first step in trying to resolve or understand a problem is the defining and limiting of the specific problem area. By defining the problem early in the discussion, the group can set certain limits if the topic is too broad for the amount of time allotted. By analyzing certain crucial terms and key concepts they are also in a better position to comprehend the scope and seriousness of the problem.

DESCRIPTION OF THE PROBLEM

Now that the members of the group have stated, defined, and limited their problem they are ready to analyze the nature of the problem. This analysis and evaluation normally demands that the participants discuss and exchange ideas and information on three topics—history of the problem, effects of the problem, and causes of the problem.

1. *History.* What has led up to a situation may offer insight into how that situation can be remedied. Whenever possible the history should extend as far forward as the STATUS QUO.

2. *Effects.* Using the various forms of support mentioned in Chapter V the group should discuss how serious the problem is and who is being affected. By reporting observed effects the members can see the outward manifestations of the problem and how widespread it is. For example, if the group was discussing "what can be done about the increased crime rate among teenagers?" someone might ask if the problem was serious; in response, another participant would attempt to substantiate the seriousness of the problem by stating that "the Governor indicated that the crime rate among teenagers in California has doubled in the last ten years." By knowing *what is happening,* (effects of the problem), the group can later decide how to remedy the problem.

3. *Causes.* The group, having examined and verified the effects of the problem, now concerns itself with the conditions which caused the effects. In deciding what caused the in-

creased crime rate (effect), someone might offer support that establishes broken homes as a cause of teenage crime.

DISCOVERY OF POSSIBLE SOLUTIONS

After the group has determined the specific problem to be solved and has examined the effects and causes of the problem, it is ready to suggest possible solutions. *All* possible solutions should be identified. Solutions suggested can be singular in nature or they can be multiple, whereby many aspects of certain solutions are combined.

Evaluation of Solutions

One of the most important characteristics of reflective thinking is the practice of withholding judgement until all possible solutions can be objectively and completely considered (a concept often referred to in the literature group processes as "suspended conclusions"). The participants should talk about each solution in detail, testing their remarks with concrete evidence, and analyzing their conclusions in light of logical reasoning. In this deliberation the advantages and disadvantages of each solution should be discussed and evaluated. How will the solution offered solve the problem? What will the solution do to the causes and effects mentioned earlier in the discussion? What will the solution do to the STATUS QUO? Once these, and other questions, have been answered, the group is ready to decide which of the solutions will best eliminate, or at least minimize, the problem. The acceptance of the "best solution" is tentative and related only to the problem mentioned in the discussion. It does not necessarily represent a decision that is fixed and static.

Plan of Action

As a final step the group must decide whether or not its preferred solution can be put into effect. If the solution seems workable, desirable and practicable, the group should determine the most effective means of implementing their findings and conclusions.

Participating in Discussion

The way in which you talk with others and make use of your information is central to the discussion process. Group interaction, personal relations and sensitivity are highly complex concepts, and can not accurately be taught in a single session or by reading a few pages of techniques. However, there are some essential tasks and responsibilities that can be learned by the participant who is motivated and willing to practice.

1. Each member of the group should be well informed on the topic. Research is *everyone's* job. Unsupported generalizations and unwarranted assertions harm the entire group.

2. Make your presence known throughout discussion. The amount of time the group has and the number of participants will obviously influence the frequency and length of your contributions, but basically you should feel free to participate as often as you have something to say.

3. See that your contributions relate to what is being said or to something that has already been said. Remarks that are simply "tossed out to the group" will often result in confusion or even force the group to depart from their established agenda.

4. Be a good listener. Common sense will tell you that most of your time in discussion is spent listening to the remarks of others. Being able to test the information used by all participants is a function of each individual in the group. If you are not attentive, you may also miss many of the relevant issues being evaluated.

5. Try to remain open minded. Your prejudices should be left outside the door. The closed mind has difficulty cooperating and objectively evaluating ideas and issues.

6. Adhere to the logical pattern selected by the group. If Dewey's reflective pattern is selected, see to it that the group "stays on the track." Jumping from effects to solutions and back to definition of terms will only waste time and frustrate the participants.

7. Try to have the contributions shared equally among all the members of the group. This means getting the timid to take part and the verbose to slow down.

8. Work for a decision by majority. Remember, cooperation is one of the key elements of successful discussion. This does not mean that honest differences have no place in group de-

liberation but rather that debate and disagreement should be over ideas and data, not over personalities.

9. Supply leadership for the group whenever needed. There is a tendency among many participants to rely solely on the judgment of the leader for decisions that are basically the responsibility of all the participants. There are, in addition, many "functions" of a leader that can easily be performed by *any* alert member of the group. For example, any participant can offer summaries whenever he feels they are appropriate and would aid the group. Don't make the mistake of assuming the leader, because he holds that title, has all of the answers.

10. Try to create an atmosphere that is conducive to constructive and purposeful discussion. A relaxed and friendly atmosphere is far more productive than one that is characterized by tension.

Leading a Discussion

If one would have the opportunity to function in the ideal or "perfect" situation, he would not have to worry about the problem of appointing a leader. The group would move systematically through the reflective process and each member would do his fair share of thinking and contributing. However, most discussions are not fortunate enough to have leadership shared among all of the members and therefore must rely on a single leader to guide the group and stimulate participation.

Research studies into group processes and group dynamics have revealed that the ability to lead a group is not something one is born with, but rather, that leadership is composed of traits that can be learned and cultivated.

1. The leader should create a cooperative, democratic climate. A group atmosphere characterized by demagoguery is less creative and quite often filled with discontent.

2. The leader should try to remain impartial whenever possible. There is a tendency among members of a group to view the leader as a "boss" or someone of superior rank. Viewed in this way, the leader who states his conclusions at the beginning of the discussion tends to close the door on free and open de-

liberation. This does not mean that the leader can not take part, it simply suggests that he sees to it that all sides get presented and that he does not become a spokesman for one point of view too early in the discussion.

3. The leader has the responsibility of getting the discussion started. This involves having the group get acquainted as well as enunciating the purpose of the meeting and stating the problem.

4. The leader should try to get general participation among all members of the group. This includes changing the communication behavior of the monopolist as well as the shy member of the group. It is the leader's encouragement and attitude which often determines the frequency of participation among the individuals in the group.

5. The leader should see that a plan, an agenda, or an organizational pattern is followed, and that the main phases of the problem get considered. If an agenda is used, it is the leader who becomes its particular guardian. In short, the leader must always be asking himself, and the participants, "Where have we been?" "Where are we now?" and "Where are we going?"

6. The leader should make abundant use of transitions and summaries. By utilizing these two techniques the leader can keep the discussion organized and also keep everyone informed as to the group's progress.

7. The leader should be sufficiently well informed on the subject. In this way he will be able to rule wisely on the relevance of contributions, answer questions, and direct the group towards the final goal.

8. The leader should try to clarify details and contributions whenever possible. If necessary, he should re-word or re-phrase a contribution. There will be occasions when he might even ask someone else to clarify the point or evidence in question.

9. The leader must try to stimulate critical thinking. A climate of questioning and skepticism is necessary if the reflective process is really going to be effective.

10. The leader should try to bring the discussion to a satisfactory conclusion. He can summarize the solution if one has been reached or can offer a summary that highlights the points

of agreement. He can also conclude the discussion by reviewing the questions and problems that still remain unanswered.

SUMMARY

In this chapter we have sought to deal with special communication situations. Although all communication is in a sense special, and therefore utilizes similarities in form and style, there are certain situations that demand a different degree of proficiency if the speaker is to accomplish his purpose. The most common of these occasions are entertaining speeches, after-dinner speeches, the impromptu speech, making introductions, and taking part in group discussion.

The major purpose of the speech to entertain is to have the listeners enjoy themselves. The speaker, by employing the concepts of attention and interest, has his audience relax in an enjoyable atmosphere. Humor is often a trade-mark of entertaining. This means that the successful speaker must learn to use the humorous illustration, exaggeration, incongruity, attacking of authority, and other such devices.

The after-dinner speech is similar to the speech to entertain. Here again the speaker strives for a light-hearted and congenial atmosphere. This speech is usually brief and "fun to listen to."

The impromptu speech is given on the "spur-of-the-moment" or when the speaker has little time to prepare. To keep from being completely over-whelmed the speaker can call forth a few simple techniques. He can remember what was said just before he was asked to speak, he can think about his past reading and speaking experiences, and he can work out a suitable organizational pattern.

The main task of the speech of introduction is to create a rapport between speaker, subject and audience. By stimulating interest in the speaker and his topic, you will create a climate which is friendly and one in which the audience is interested in hearing what the guest speaker has to say.

In this day of group consciousness we are constantly being asked to solve problems by means of group discussion. The discussant may find himself in a lecture-forum, symposium, panel or informal discussion. In all of these situations it is important for the participants to be well informed and well organized. For once the subject has been located and worded it must be analyzed and evaluated. Dewey's five steps of reflective thinking constitutes one organizational scheme which is quite helpful in solving problems. Finally, each member, whether participant or leader, should take part, be well informed, should cooperate, listen, follow an organizational plan, and try to stimulate contributions from all of the other members.

SUGGESTED READINGS

J. Jeffery Auer, *Essentials of Parliamentary Procedure*, (New York: Appleton-Century-Crofts, Inc., 1959).

James T. Baker, *The Short Speech*, (Englewood Cliffs, N. J.: Prentice-Hall, Inc., 1938). Chapters 6-8.

D. C. Barnlund, and F. S. Haiman, *The Dynamics of Discussion*, (Boston: Houghton Mifflin Company, 1960).

Jacob Braude, *Braude's Handbook of Humor for all Occasions*, (New York: Prentice-Hall, Inc., 1959).

Laura Crowell, *Discussion: Method of Democracy*, (Chicago: Scott, Foresman and Company, 1964).

Halbert E. Gulley, *Discussion, Conference, and Group Process*, (New York: Holt, Rinehart, and Winston, Inc., 1960).

R. Victor Harnack, and Thorrel B. Fest, *Group Discussion, Theory and Technique*, (New York: Appleton-Century-Crofts, Inc., 1964).

Stewart Harral, *When It's Laughter You're After*, (Oklahoma: University of Oklahoma Press, 1962).

William S. Howell, and Donald K. Smith, *Discussion*, (New York: The Macmillan Company, 1956).

James H. McBurney, and Kenneth G. Hance, *Discussion in Human Affairs*, (New York: Harper and Brothers, 1950).

William M. Sattler, and N. Edd Miller, *Discussion and Conference*, (Englewood Cliffs, N. J.: Prentice-Hall, Inc., 1954).

Andrew T. Weaver, and Ordean G. Ness, *An Introduction to Public Speaking*, (New York: The Odyssey Press, Inc., 1961). Chapter 7.

W. Hayes Yeager, *Effective Speaking for Every Occasion*, (Englewood Cliffs, N. J.: Prentice-Hall, Inc., 1951). Chapter 10.

APPENDIX

SPEECH EVALUATION SCALE

Speaker_____ Date _____

Subject_____ Round_____

SPEECH PROCESSES	RATINGS AND COMMENTS

CONTENT: Purpose, thesis, analysis:
  Specific purpose: clear___
    narrowed ___ appropriate to
    audience ___
  Thesis: clear___ narrowed ___
    appropriate to audience ___
    speaker___
  Analysis of thesis: accurate ___
    thorough ___
  Main points: directly support
    thesis ___ fully develop
    thesis ___
	1 2 3 4 5

CONTENT: Development
  Supporting material: clear ___
    relevant ___ specific ___
    adequate in amount ___ interesting ___
  Logical reasoning: accurate ___
    supported ___
  Facts: clear___ relevant ___
    adequate ___ interesting ___
  Statistics: clear ___ relevant___
    adequate ___ correctly interpreted ___ interesting ___
  Examples: clear___ adequate___
    interesting ___
  Testimony: clear___ adequate___
    interesting ___
	1 2 3 4 5

ORGANIZATION:
    clear ___ effective ___
  Introduction: gets attention ___
    orients ___ thesis stated ___
    partition ___ creates interest ___ proper subordination ___
  Body:
    Main points: clear ___ patterned ___
    Sub-points: clear ___ patterned ___
  Conclusion: summary ___ effective ___
  Transitions: smooth___
    clear ___ signposts___
	1 2 3 4 5

219

LANGUAGE:
  Grammar: appropriate level __
    errors __
  Rhetorical qualities: oral
    style __ clear __ appropri-
    ate __ interesting __ con-
    crete __
	1 2 3 4 5

DELIVERY:
  Physical presentation: appear-
    ance __ poise __ enthusi-
    asm __ directness __ eye
    contact __ posture __ ges-
    tures __ facial expres-
    sion __
  Oral presentation: articula-
    tion __ fluency __ pronuncia-
    tion __ variety __ pitch __
    rate __ loudness __ direct-
    ness __
	1 2 3 4 5

SPEECH OUTLINE	1 2 3 4 5

Item markings:
    +   —very good
(no mark)—average or better
    ✓   —needs improvement

RATINGS:
5 very good
4 good
3 average
2 poor
1 unsatisfactory

SPEECH EVALUATION

I. DELIVERY

    A. Eye contact   good _____
- 1. aimless _____   3. windows _____
- 2. floor _____   4. other _____ .

    B. Posture   good _____
- 1. stiff _____   3. aimless movement _____
- 2. shifting of weight ____   4. other _____ .

    C. Gestures   good _____
- 1. need more _____   3. poor timing _____
- 2. larger _____   4. other _____ .

    D. Vocal variety   good _____
- 1. change and vary your   2. pause _____
  - a. rate _____   3. enthusiasm _____
  - b. force _____   4. other _____ .
  - c. pitch _____
  - d. volume _____

II. CONTENT

    A. Audience analysis   good _____
- 1. topic too general ____   2. not for this audience _____
- 3. "feedback" _____
- 4. other _____ .

    B. Imagery and Wording   good _____
- 1. more detail _____   2. poor word choice _____
- 3. other _____ .

    C. Support and evidence   good _____
- 1. old sources _____   2. unrelated to issue _____
- 3. weak __ , because _____ .

    D. Motivation (Motive appeals)   good _____
- 1. poor audience analysis ____   3. more development ____
- 2. more detail _____   4. other _____ .

    E. Introduction   good _____
        weak, because _____ .

    F. Organization   good _____
- 1. no clear pattern _____
- 2. weak, because _____ .

III. OTHER

SPEECH TO CONVINCE

SPEAKER _____

RATING SCALE: 5—Superior; 4—Above Average; 3—Average;
    2—Fair; 1—Poor.

INTRODUCTION (circle one)   5 4 3 2 1

    Did the opening words get favorable attention?

    Was the issue under contention introduced tactfully?

    Did the speaker make you feel that the issue was worth considering?

BODY   5 4 3 2 1

    Was the central idea (proposition) clear?

    Were the purpose and central idea sufficiently narrowed?

    Did the main points suffice to prove the central idea?

    Were there too many main points? too few? satisfactory number?

    Was each main point supported by evidence?

    Were sources of evidence cited?

    Did the evidence meet the tests of credibility?

    Was the reasoning from the evidence sound?

    Was the speech adapted to audience interests?

    Was the speech adapted to existing audience attitudes toward the topic?

CONCLUSION   5 4 3 2 1

    Did the conclusion focus the whole speech on the central idea?

LANGUAGE USAGE   5 4 3 2 1

    Clear?

    Correct?

    Appropriate?

    Vivid?

DELIVERY   5 4 3 2 1

    Visual:

    Vocal:

        DOMINANT IMPRESSION OF THE SPEECH _____

PROPOSITION OF POLICY

SPEAKER _____

RATING SCALE: 5—Superior; 4—Above Average; 3—Average;
    2—Fair; 1—Poor.

HOW CONVINCINGLY DOES THE SPEAKER SHOW:

That a problem exists? _____

That it is significant enough to warrant correction? _____

That it is caused by an inherent weakness in the
present system? _____

That the proposed solution will correct the problem? _____

That the solution will be feasible? _____

That any disadvantages will be outweighed by
advantages? _____

That the proposed solution is the best solution
to the problem? _____

HOW EFFECTIVELY DOES THE SPEAKER EMPLOY:

Evidence of fact and/or opinion? _____

    (Underline any appropriate categories: Evidence
    was insufficient in quantity; poor in quality;
    improperly applied; not clearly related to the
    point supposedly being proved; sources not given;
    credibility of sources not always established)

Forms of reasoning? _____

    (Underline any appropriate categories: Faulty
    reasoning from examples; from axiom, from cause
    to probable effect; from effect to probable cause;
    from analogy)

Factors of attention and interest? _____

Signposts for organizational clarity? _____

Language? _____

Visual aspects of delivery? _____

Vocal aspects of delivery? _____

    DOMINANT IMPRESSION OF THE SPEECH _____

SPEECH TO INFORM

SPEAKER _____

RATING SCALE:

  5-superior; 4-above average; 3-average; 2-fair; 1-poor

CHOICE OF SUBJECT   _____

INTRODUCTION

  Opening statements effectively gain attention?   _____

  Did the speaker make you feel a need for information? _____

  Did he establish his right to inform, directly or indirectly? _____

  Graceful transition into the body of the speech?   _____

BODY

  Clarity of organization?   _____

  Information made interesting?   _____

  Information made understandable?   _____

  Visual aid handled capably?   _____

CONCLUSION

  Speech gracefully concluded?   _____

LANGUAGE USAGE

  Clear?   _____

  Grammatically correct?

  Vivid?   _____

  Appropriate?   _____

USE OF VOICE (Check the appropriate blank)

  Pitch level: Too high ____ Too low ____ OK _____

  Variation of pitch: Varied ____ Monotonous to a degree _____

  Very monotonous _____

  Rate: Too fast ____ Too slow ____ OK _____

  Variation of rate: Too little ____ Too much ____ OK ____

  Loudness: Too loud ____ Too soft ____ OK _____

  Variation of Loudness: Too little ____ Too much ____ OK ____

  Pronunciation: Generally correct ____ Frequently faulty _____

  Words mispronounced: _____

  Enunciation (distinctness): Clear ____ Slurring _____

VISUAL ASPECTS OF DELIVERY

  Posture: Alert but at ease ____ All weight on one foot _____

  Leaning on lectern ____ Stiff ____ Shifting weight constantly_____

  Gestures: Too few ____ Too many ____ OK in quantity_____

  Quality of gestures: Properly motivated ____ Affected _____

  Clumsy _____

  Movements: Immobile ____ Distracting movements ____ Satisfac-

  tory in quantity and quality _____

  Facial Expression: Very animated ____ Occasionally animated _____

  Never animated _____

  Eye Contacts: Looked at everyone ____ Favored one section _____

  Avoided audience _____

TOTAL IMPRESSION LEFT BY SPEECH (Use rating scale) _____

EVALUATION AND CRITICISM OF SPEECHES

1. Has the speaker made an attempt to be objective and fair to himself, the audience, and the subject?

2. Did the speaker have a worthwhile purpose? Was it of college caliber? Was the purpose easy to follow and logically developed?

3. Was there evidence that the speaker had analyzed his audience and his speaking occasion?

4. Did the speaker know his subject? Did he seem to be prepared both in terms of research and in terms of oral practice?

5. Was the speech structurally sound? Did the subdivisions, both major and minor, relate to and support the main ideas? Were the transitions between ideas clear?

6. Did the speaker utilize language meaningfully? Did he employ words or phrases that were clear and adequately defined? Did he make effective use of imagery and word pictures? Did he avoid cliches, slang, and poor grammar? Was his usage appropriate to the audience, the occasion, and the subject?

7. Did the speaker utilize factors of attention and interest in both the content and delivery of the speech?

8. Did the speaker's illustrations, examples, statistics, testimony and analogies meet the tests of sound evidence? Was enough evidence employed to support each point?

9. Did the speaker reflect a "sense of communication?" Did he maintain eye contact? Did he employ vocal variety? Was there adequate movement?

10. What was the total impression left by the speech?

11. How successfully did the speaker fulfill the demands of the specific speech assignment?

ONE-POINT OUTLINE

General Purpose: To convince
Specific Response: Driving after drinking is dangerous

I. Driving after drinking is dangerous.

    A. Gareth Martinis, 29, went driving after drinking last May 19.

        1. He was driving on a New York suburb street.
        2. He was drunk and speeding.
        3. He hit the rear of the auto in front of him.

(factual
illustration)

            a. The auto he hit went into the oncoming lane of traffic.
            b. The car hit another automobile head-on.
            c. Five people were killed because of Gareth's drinking.

    B. Many other serious accidents are the direct result of drivers who had been drinking.

(specific
instances)

        1. In Madison, Connecticut, four drunk friends went driving 60 mph eastward in the westbound lane of the Connecticut turnpike, killing five people.
        2. A drunk driver proving to a hitchhiker he could do 110 mph killed himself and the hitchhiker.
        3. In El Cajon several months ago, a woman who had been drinking hit and killed an elderly pedestrian in a crosswalk.

    C. Numerous studies indicate driving after drinking is dangerous.

(statistics)

        1. The New York State Board of Health issued a report stating that 73% of the fatal accidents in New York City were caused by drivers who had been drinking.
           ("New York study: links Drivers' Deaths to Drinking," American City, Vol. 76, March 1965, pp. 59-63.)
        2. The Montana Highway Patrol examined blood samples from all drivers killed in autos in their state and found 48.6% of them were drunk at the time of the accident. ("Driver Had Been Drinking," Science Digest, Vol. 51, April, 1966, pp. 57-60.)

D. Among experts expressing their view on driving after drinking is Dr. W. H. Haddon, director of Driver Research Center of the New York State Board of Health, who has stated. . .

(testimony)
    1. "Over 50% of the United States' fatal highway automobile accidents could be prevented if the driver had not been drinking before-hand." ("Drunk Driving," Popular Science, Vol. 178, March 1963, pp. 85–87.)

E. Driving after drinking is like driving with your eyes shut.

(analogy)
    1. The driver does not know what he is doing.
    2. The driver who has been drinking is blinded by the effects of the alcohol.
    3. You will be a much safer driver if you do your drinking after driving and not before.

II. Drinking before driving is dangerous.

(restatement)

BIBLIOGRAPHY

"Driver Had Been Drinking," Science Digest, Vol. 51, April, 1966, pp. 57-60.

"Drunk Driving," Popular Science, Vol. 178, March, 1963, pp. 85-87.

"New York Study Links Drivers' Deaths to Drinking," American City, Vol. 76, March, 1965, pp. 59-63.

UNDERSTANDING YOUR RECEIVER

The following factors are just a few of the characteristics that will influence an audience's perception and response to your message. (The term "audience" is used in this context to stand for one receiver or a large audience.)

Age _____ Sex _____ Approximately how many _____

Educational level _____ Occupation _____

Economic status _____ Group allegiances _____

_____

Political affiliation _____ Attitude toward me _____

Attitude toward the communication situation _____

Knowledge of the specific subject _____

Primary interests _____

Primary goals _____

Primary attitudes and beliefs _____

_____

Other important data _____

_____

_____

_____

EVALUATING GROUP DISCUSSION

1. How effective was the group in accomplishing its <u>overall objective</u>?

1	2	3	4	5	6	7
very effective			moderately effective			not effective

2. Did the members of the group seem <u>well prepared</u>?

1	2	3	4	5	6	7
very well prepared			moderately prepared		not at all prepared	

3. Did the group follow an <u>organizational pattern</u>?

1	2	3	4	5	6	7
very well organized		moderately organized			poorly organized	

4. Was there an effective <u>flow of communication</u> between all participants in the discussion? Comment and evaluate.

5. What were the strong and/or weak points of the group in the area of <u>participation</u>?

6. What were the strong and/or weak points of the group in the area of <u>leadership</u>?

OUT-OF-CLASS LISTENING REPORT

Supply the information requested below regarding a speech you heard presented before a religious, civic, or academic group, etc. Hand this report to your instructor during the first class meeting following the speaking event. DO NOT COMPLETE THE REPORT DURING THE SPEECH.

1. Speaker's name _____ Subject _____

2. General end _____ Specific purpose _____

3. Occasion _____ Time _____ Place _____

4. Type of audience _____ Number _____

5. How effective was he in beginning and ending his speech? _____

_____

6. List the major points developed in the speech _____

_____

7. How was the speaker's delivery? _____

_____

_____

_____

8. Did the speaker adapt his speech to this audience? (explain) _____

_____

9. Did he prove (or explain if informative speech) his main points? (explain) _____

_____

_____

10. Criticize his language in terms of clarity, interest, ambiguity, etc.

_____

_____

11. Did the speaker achieve his purpose? _____ Why or why not ___

_____

Note: Use the other side of the paper if needed.

INDEX